EVOLVE

WORKBOOK

Octavio Ramírez Espinosa

2

CAMBRIDGE
UNIVERSITY PRESS

Shaftesbury Road, Cambridge CB2 8EA, United Kingdom

One Liberty Plaza, 20th Floor, New York, NY 10006, USA

477 Williamstown Road, Port Melbourne, VIC 3207, Australia

314–321, 3rd Floor, Plot 3, Splendor Forum, Jasola District Centre, New Delhi – 110025, India

103 Penang Road, #05–06/07, Visioncrest Commercial, Singapore 238467

Cambridge University Press & Assessment is a department of the University of Cambridge.

We share the University's mission to contribute to society through the pursuit of education, learning and research at the highest international levels of excellence.

www.cambridge.org
Information on this title: www.cambridge.org/9781108408981

© Cambridge University Press & Assessment 2019

This publication is in copyright. Subject to statutory exception and to the provisions of relevant collective licensing agreements, no reproduction of any part may take place without the written permission of Cambridge University Press & Assessment.

First published 2019

20 19 18 17 16 15 14 13 12 11 10 9

Printed in Great Britain by CPI Group (UK) Ltd, Croydon CR0 4YY

A catalogue record for this publication is available from the British Library

ISBN 978-1-108-40524-9 Student's Book
ISBN 978-1-108-40505-8 Student's Book A
ISBN 978-1-108-40917-9 Student's Book B
ISBN 978-1-108-40526-3 Student's Book with Practice Extra
ISBN 978-1-108-40506-5 Student's Book with Practice Extra A
ISBN 978-1-108-40919-3 Student's Book with Practice Extra B
ISBN 978-1-108-40898-1 Workbook with Audio
ISBN 978-1-108-40863-9 Workbook with Audio A
ISBN 978-1-108-41192-9 Workbook with Audio B
ISBN 978-1-108-40516-4 Teacher's Edition with Test Generator
ISBN 978-1-108-41065-6 Presentation Plus
ISBN 978-1-108-41202-5 Class Audio CDs
ISBN 978-1-108-40788-5 Video Resource Book with DVD
ISBN 978-1-108-41446-3 Full Contact with DVD
ISBN 978-1-108-41153-0 Full Contact with DVD A
ISBN 978-1-108-41412-8 Full Contact with DVD B

Additional resources for this publication at www.cambridge.org/evolve

Cambridge University Press & Assessment has no responsibility for the persistence or accuracy of URLs for external or third-party internet websites referred to in this publication and does not guarantee that any content on such websites is, or will remain, accurate or appropriate. Information regarding prices, travel timetables, and other factual information given in this work is correct at the time of first printing but Cambridge University Press & Assessment does not guarantee the accuracy of such information thereafter.

CONTENTS

1 VOCABULARY: Describing people you know

A **Write the connection you have with each person: FAM (Family), FR (Friend or Romantic), W/S (Work or School).**

1	FR	boyfriend
2		boss
3		brother
4		classmate
5		close friend
6		girlfriend
7		grandchild
8		grandfather
9		neighbor
10		roommate

B **Where possible, write the name of a person you know next to each connection in exercise A.**

2 GRAMMAR: *be*; possessive adjectives

A **Complete the text with the correct form of the verb *be*.**

My name ¹ is Raul, and I ² _____ from Mexico.
I'm an English teacher now in Miami, Florida. These ³ _____
the people in my life. My grandparents ⁴ _____ Monica and
Roberto – that's them in the photo. This is their house in Valle de Bravo,
Mexico. My brothers' names ⁵ _____ Sergio and Raymundo.
We ⁶ _____ very close friends. This ⁷ _____
a photo of me with Marisela. People always ask, ⁸" _____
she your girlfriend?" No, she ⁹ _____ not!
She ¹⁰ _____ my neighbor.

B **Match the columns.**

1	I	**a**	_____	their	
2	you	**b**	_____	his	
3	he	**c**	_____	our	
4	she	**d**	_____	her	
5	it	**e**	_____	your	
6	we	**f**	_1_	my	
7	they	**g**	_____	its	

3 GRAMMAR AND VOCABULARY

A **Complete the questions for a social media profile. Then answer the questions.**

1 What _____is_____ your name?

_____

2 Where _____ you from?

_____

3 What _____ your classmates' names?

_____

4 _____ they your friends?

_____

5 What _____ your close friend's name?

_____

6 _____ he or she your roommate?

_____

7 What _____ your boyfriend or girlfriend's name?

_____

8 _____ she or he from Canada?

_____

B **Complete the sentences with the correct possessive adjective.**

his	her	its	~~my~~	our	their	your

1 I have a pen. This is _____my_____ pen.
2 My boyfriend has a new car. This is _____ new car.
3 Is this _____ girlfriend? Are you close friends?
4 Marie lives near my family. She is _____ neighbor.
5 Carol and Sissy are my roommates. That is _____ room.
6 The dog is hungry. This is _____ food.
7 She is the new boss. _____ name is Ms. Singh.

1.2 WHAT'S IN YOUR BAG?

1 VOCABULARY: Naming everyday things

A Write the words in the correct column. What things can you put in your pocket? What things can't you put in your pocket?

candy bar	cash	driver's license	gum	hairbrush	hand lotion
keychain	mirror	receipt	~~tissues~~	umbrella	water bottle

In my pocket	Not in my pocket
tissues	

2 GRAMMAR: Possession

A Circle the correct words to complete the conversation.

Teacher Excuse me, class. Who's / *Whose* jacket is this?

Girl It isn't *mine / ours. My / Your* jacket has pockets.

Teacher Tyler, is this *yours / whose*?

Boy No. It isn't *mine / his. Mine / My* jacket is green.

Teacher Oh, look! Here's a name in the jacket. It belongs to Sarah. It's *hers / his*.

Boy Sarah, it's *her / your* jacket.

Sarah No, it isn't. It belongs to a different Sarah. *Mine / Yours* is blue.

B Circle the words that are not correct in the conversation. Then correct the mistakes.

Man Excuse me. I think that's (mine) wife's keychain. _____

Woman No, sorry, it isn't her. _____

Man Are you sure? I think it belong to her. _____

Woman No, it's mine. It belongs me. _____

Man Oh, I see. You're right. So where's his wife's keychain? _____

Woman Look! There's another keychain on the desk. Is that his? _____

Man No, that isn't her. _____

3 GRAMMAR AND VOCABULARY

A **Circle the correct answer to complete the questions.**

1 _____ mirror is that?

  (a) Whose   **b** Who   **c** Where

2 _____ that umbrella yours?

  a Is   **b** Are   **c** Whose

3 Whose cash _____ that?

  a are   **b** am   **c** is

4 _____ those tissues yours?

  a Is   **b** Are   **c** Whose

5 _____ candy bar is that?

  a Who   **b** Where   **c** Whose

6 _____ driver's license is that?

  a Whose   **b** Who's   **c** What

7 Does that gum _____ him?

  a belongs to   **b** belong to   **c** belong

8 Is that keychain _____ ?

  a our   **b** our's   **c** ours

B **Answer the questions in exercise A based on the diagram below.**

1 *That mirror is ours. / That's our mirror.*   5 _____

2 _____   6 _____

3 _____   7 _____

4 _____   8 _____

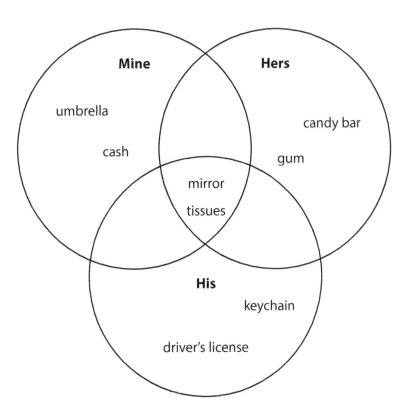

5

HOW DO YOU KNOW RAQUEL?

1 FUNCTIONAL LANGUAGE: Greeting someone and starting conversations

A   Complete the conversation with the phrases in the box.

~~Are you~~	Great to meet you, too	Great to see you again
It's really good to see you	Long time, no see	Pleased to meet you

Anna   Good morning! ¹ _____ Are you _____ Lauren?

Lauren   Yes, I am.

Anna   ² _____. I'm Anna. It's my first day. I'm on Joe's team.

Lauren   Welcome, Anna! ³ _____. I want to introduce you to my assistant. This is Peter.

Anna   I know Peter. Hi, ⁴ _____.

Peter   ⁵ _____, Anna.
              ⁶ _____ !

Anna   Yes, almost two years.

Lauren   Well, I'm glad we all know each other now.

2 REAL-WORLD STRATEGY: Showing interest and surprise

A   Put the conversation in order.

☐ **George**   Wow! Hey, Neil! Long time, no see!

1 **Neil**   Good morning. I'm Neil. Are you James?

☐ **Neil**   Yes, I know George from a long time ago. It's really great to see you.

☐ **James**   Yes, I am. Hi, Neil. Pleased to meet you.

☐ **James**   Wait … do you know each other?

☐ **Neil**   Great to meet you, too. It's my first day in sales.

☐ **James**   Seriously? George is an old friend of mine, too. This is great!

☐ **James**   Is it really? OK. Well, this is George, he's a manager. George, this is Neil, he's a new salesperson.

3   FUNCTIONAL LANGUAGE AND REAL-WORLD STRATEGY

A   **Complete the conversation with your own information.**

Carlos	I'm Carlos. Pleased to meet you.
Me	Hi, I'm [1]_____ . Great [2]_____ .
Carlos	I recognize you from English class. It's [3]_____ .
Me	[4]_____ ? Oh, yeah, I remember you, too. Is this your first time in this class?
Carlos	Yes, it is.
Me	Great! This is my friend, [5]_____ . [6]_____ , this is Carlos.
[7]_____	Hi, Carlos. [8]_____ .
Carlos	Hey, [9]_____ . [10]_____ , too.
Me	Wait … do you know each other?
Carlos	Yes, we take other classes together.
Me	[11]_____ ? That's awesome!

7

1.4 EMAIL INTRODUCTIONS

1 READING

A **Read the email and label the parts.**

Reason for writing: R	Greeting: G
End of mail: E	Closing: C
Full name: F	Introduction: I
Subject: S	

Reply   Forward

_S_	**Re: Cars**
_____	Dear Thomas,
_____	My name is Anton Taft. Your cousin, Sarah Griffin, is my friend.
_____	Do you like old cars? I repair them! It's my hobby. I have a car from 1958. Attached is a photo.
_____	Please call me at 202-555-4646. We can meet on Saturday and you can see the car.
_____	Thanks!
_____	Anton Taft

2 LISTENING

A 🔊 **1.01** **LISTEN FOR DETAIL** **Listen to the voicemail message. Number the sentences in the order you hear them.**

☐ I want to give you some information about the summer schedule. All departments follow the new schedule starting next week. The summer schedule is in this morning's email.

☐ My name is Cindy Clark, head of the human resources department.

☐ Hello, Mr. Chen,

☐ Let me know if there are any questions.

☐ Thank you!

8

A **Put the parts of the email in the correct order.**

☐ I want to invite you to our first neighbors' meeting. Please find the agenda for the meeting included with this letter. The meeting is at my house.

☐ Rick Lock

☐ Dear Mrs. Albertson,

☐ My name is Rick Lock. I'm a neighbor of yours. Welcome to the neighborhood.

☐ Sincerely,

☐ Thank you very much for your time. I look forward to seeing you at the meeting.

☐ Re: Upcoming meeting

B **Complete the email with your own ideas.**

● ● ●   Reply   Forward   ✉

Re: New weekend classes

1 _____ Mick,

I'm Roger from the gym. 2 _____ ?
I hope everything is great for you!

I want to invite you to my special dance classes on Saturdays and Sundays. We are starting
3 _____ . Please see the calendar included with this email.

I hope 4 _____ us.

5 _____ ,

Roger Strong

CHECK AND REVIEW

Read the statements. Can you do these things?

UNIT 1	Mark the boxes. ✔ I can do it. ? I am not sure. I can …	If you are not sure, go back to these pages in the Student's Book.
VOCABULARY	☐ talk about people I know. ☐ name everyday things.	page 2 page 4
GRAMMAR	☐ use *be*. ☐ use possessive adjectives.	page 3 page 5
FUNCTIONAL LANGUAGE	☐ greet people and start a conversation. ☐ show interest and surprise.	page 6 page 7
SKILLS	☐ introduce myself in an email. ☐ use capital letters.	page 9 page 9

1   VOCABULARY: Expressions with *do*, *have*, and *make*

A   **Complete the actions with *do, have,* or *make*.**

have	a party	_____	a snack
_____	free time	_____	housework
_____	plans	_____	something to drink
_____	some work	_____	the bed
_____	the dishes	_____	the laundry

B   **Write the phrases in exercise A in the correct column. Are there phrases that go in both columns?**

Tasks	Fun

2   GRAMMAR: Simple present for habits and routines

A   **Complete the sentences with the correct form of the verbs in parentheses.**

1 I _____ _don't have_ _____ (not have) much free time tomorrow.

2 We always _____ (have) a party for my birthday.

3 _____ they _____ (do sleep) for eight hours every night? No, they _____ (do).

4 He usually _____ (have) something to drink with dinner.

5 She _____ (do) the dishes and then _____ (have) a snack every day.

6 Sam _____ (not make) plans for after work.

7 My roommate _____ (not make) his bed but he _____ (do) the laundry every week.

8 Ben _____ (usually do) the housework. I _____ (not do) the housework, but I _____ (always do) the laundry.

B **Correct the sentences.**

1 They often in the afternoon do the dishes.

They often do the dishes in the afternoon.

2 I don't on Mondays do the laundry.

_____

3 Julia makes plans with her mom at night sometimes.

_____

4 Peter and I have something to drink often with dinner.

_____

5 When do you have free time usually?

_____

6 How does he do housework often?

_____

7 Every morning I do some work on my computer.

_____

8 We have a snack never before dinner.

_____

3 GRAMMAR AND VOCABULARY

A **Write the names of the people in your home who do the following actions. Then write when they do it.**

| do the dishes | do housework | do the laundry |
| have a snack | make plans | make the bed |

What	Who	When
do the dishes	my …	every …

B **Write sentences using the information in exercise A.**

1 My sister usually does the dishes every Saturday.

2 _____

3 _____

4 _____

5 _____

6 _____

2.2 WHERE'S YOUR WORKSPACE?

1 VOCABULARY: Naming work and study items

A **Cross out the word that is different.**

1 mouse	~~textbook~~	Wi-Fi	keyboard
2 document	files	note	outlet
3 keyboard	calendar	computer	mouse
4 home	office	school	document
5 files	calendar	textbook	headphones
6 calendar	keyboard	files	document

B **Label the pictures below with words in exercise A.**

_____

_____

_____

_____

_____

_____

2 GRAMMAR: *This / that one; these / those ones*

A **Circle the correct words to complete the sentences.**

1 I like to clean my office every week. You see all *these* / *those* papers here on my desk? They are documents that I usually keep in *that / this* cabinet over there. But I'm working on many jobs now, so I have all of them here for the moment.

2 I share this office with Tim. He likes to listen to music. *Those ones / Those* are his headphones on his chair. I usually sit by the window. I watch people buy their newspapers at *that / this* newsstand on the corner.

3 We have many laptops in our office. *This one / This* is my favorite. I like it because the keyboard is big. It has a wider screen than *these / those* by the door. I usually use it.

12

B   Ask the people in the pictures about the objects. Complete your questions and their answers. Use *this*, *that*, *these*, or *those*, and *this / that one* or *these / those ones*.

1 A What is _____ ?
   B _____ is my table.
2 A Is _____ your favorite umbrella?
   B Yes, it's _____ _____ .
3 A What are _____ ?
   B _____ are Tim and Laura's chairs.
4 A _____ desk is where I usually work.
   B It's bigger than _____ over there.

3 GRAMMAR AND VOCABULARY

A   **Look at the picture. Circle the correct answers about the things in the picture.**

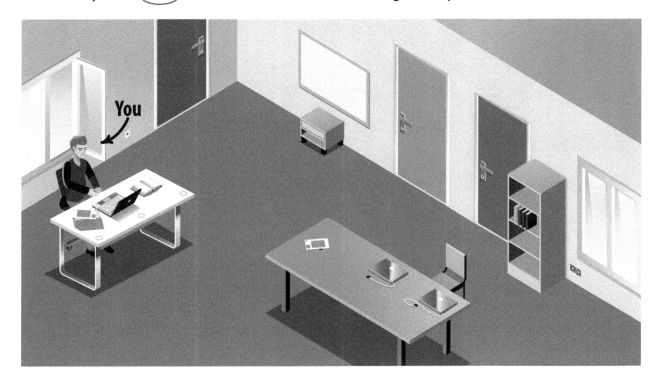

1 *This is / These are* an open laptop. *That one / Those ones* aren't open.
2 *This / These* documents *is / are* on the desk. *That one / Those ones is / are* on the table.
3 *This is / These are* a modern desk. *That is / Those are* a table.
4 *This is / These are* an open window. *That one isn't / Those ones aren't* open.

B   **Choose other things in the picture. Write sentences like the ones in exercise A using *this / that one* and *these / those*.**

_____   _____

_____   _____

THE CONNECTION'S TERRIBLE

1 FUNCTIONAL LANGUAGE: Explaining communication problems

A   **Put the conversation in order.**

☐1 **Maria**   Hi, Julio. How are you?

☐ **Maria**   OK … How about now? Julio? Are you still there?

☐ **Maria**   Hm … I think it's my Wi-Fi. Let me see … Is that any better?

☐ **Maria**   Hm … Let me call you again, OK?

☐ **Maria**   I can't. I have meetings all day. Let me change my mic … How about now?

☐ **Julio**   Uh, … It's not better, sorry. The echo is still there.

☐ **Julio**   Hi. Maria? Sorry, I can't hear you very well.

☐ **Julio**   No, I'm sorry. Maria, you're breaking up. The connection is terrible

☐ **Julio**   Yes, I'm still here, but there's an echo now. Can we try again later today?

☐ **Julio**   OK. Thanks.

2 REAL-WORLD STRATEGY: Asking for repetition and confirmation

A Match the columns to complete the questions.

1	Sorry, I …	a	_____	any better?
2	Can you …	b	_____	hear me OK?
3	Are you …	c	_____	about now?
4	Sorry, can …	d	_____	didn't catch that.
5	How …	e	_____	still there?
6	Is that …	f	_____	you say that again?

3 FUNCTIONAL LANGUAGE AND REAL-WORLD STRATEGY

A Write a phone conversation that describes a problem with a bad phone connection. Before you write the conversation, complete the chart with the situation and the expressions you plan to use.

Situation	
Explaining the problem	
Checking the problem	
Solving the problem	
Asking for repetition	

B Write the conversation using the expressions in exercise A.

A Hi. _____

B _____

A _____

B _____

A _____

B _____

A _____

B _____

1 LISTENING

A 🔊 **2.01** Listen to the podcast. (Circle) the correct answers.

1 What does Ada do after breakfast?

    a She calls clients.   **b** She writes stories.   **c** She uses her computer.

2 Why does she like her workspace?

    a It has a big table.   **b** She can make lots of coffee.

    c There is a lot of light.

3 How does she work?

    a on her laptop   **b** on her tablet   **c** with pen and paper

4 What is the interview about?

    a being successful   **b** daily habits   **c** fame and fortune

B 🔊 **2.01** **LISTEN FOR DETAIL** Listen to the podcast again. Match the columns to complete the sentences.

1 Ada usually   _____   **a** after she writes down her ideas.

2 The room where she works   _____   **b** plans a new book.

3 She writes new notes   _____   **c** writes more than 1,000 words a day.

4 She never   _____   **d** is her favorite place in the house.

5 She uses her computer   _____   **e** on paper.

2 READING

A **Read the magazine article.** (Circle) the correct answers to complete the sentences.

Lessons in Life

Damian Brand offers four lessons to help you with your career choices.

There is a famous quotation by American inventor and businessman Thomas Alva Edison (1847–1931): "Genius is 1% inspiration and 99% perspiration." So, lesson number one: if you want something in life, you need to work really hard for it.

Lesson in life number two: do what you love. If your job is about something you really like, you have a very good start. I believe that people who work hard are people who usually love their jobs.

Lesson number three: know what you want to achieve and how you can achieve it. My advice is to make a list of goals and practical things you can do to achieve them.

Lesson four: believe in your talents, and don't give up. It's easy to think that employers don't want you or what you can do. But your big break is just around the corner …

1 This article says that success is *easy / hard* work.

2 It helps if you *enjoy / don't like* what you do.

3 Goals *help / invite* you to be successful.

4 Don't stop *working / playing*.

B   **Read the article again. Circle the correct answers.**

1   What does Thomas Edison's quotation mean? It means it's important to …
    a   have talent.   b   work hard.   c   have talent and work hard.

2   Why does Damian think that people work hard? Because they …
    a   don't have a choice.   b   love their jobs.   c   make a lot of money.

3   What is Damian's advice about career goals?
    a   Have goals you can achieve.   b   Make a list of jobs you want.   c   Have big dreams.

3   WRITING

A   **Read the following statements. Give your opinion about them using the phrases in the box.**

another example	for example	I don't believe	like all others	very interesting

1   All famous businesspeople are successful.

    I don't believe all famous businesspeople are successful. For example …

2   All successful people are very organized.

    _____

3   Successful people play sports and have interesting habits.

    _____

4   You need to earn a lot of money to become successful.

    _____

5   Success is about having a lot of people work for you.

    _____

B   **Write a blog entry about your daily habits and how you think they help you become a successful person. Include as many examples as possible.**

CHECK AND REVIEW

Read the statements. Can you do these things?

UNIT 2	Mark the boxes. ☑ I can do it. ？ I am not sure. I can …	If you are not sure, go back to these pages in the Student's Book.
VOCABULARY	☐ use expressions with *do, have,* and *make.* ☐ name work and study items.	page 12 page 14
GRAMMAR	☐ use the simple present to describe habits and routines. ☐ use *this / that one; these / those ones* to talk about objects near and far.	page 13 page 15
FUNCTIONAL LANGUAGE	☐ talk about communication problems. ☐ ask someone to repeat something.	page 16 page 17
SKILLS	☐ write my opinion of a podcast. ☐ use correct spelling.	page 19 page 19

UNIT 3   LET'S MOVE

3.1   WE'RE WINNING!

1 VOCABULARY: Sports

Across:

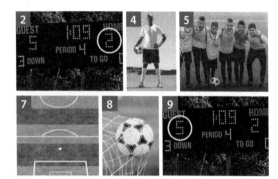

Down:

A   Look at the pictures and complete the crossword.

B   Complete the sentences. Use the correct form of the words from the crossword in exercise A.

1   Many _____fans_____ are excited to see their team play tonight.

2   The _____ is full! There are so many people exercising!

3   There is my favorite soccer _____! Hi, Cristiano!

4   Del Potro is a great Argentinian tennis player! He is _____ _____ the set, 30–20.

5   I love tennis! Look! Serena Williams is on the _____ now!

6   Wait! There are only nine players on the soccer _____.

7   The swimmers are jumping into the _____.

8   Chile is _____ to the other _____! Argentina is going to win!

9   The Australian runners are winning the 1,600-meter _____!

18

2 GRAMMAR: Present continuous

A **Complete the sentences using the present continuous. Use the pictures to help you.**

1 She _____ (talk) to the man.

2 He _____ (have) a drink of water.

3 They _____ (talk) together.

4 Laverne and Marconie _____ (win).

B **Look at the pictures. What is each picture about? Write a sentence about each one.**

1 _____   2 _____   3 _____   4 _____

3 GRAMMAR AND VOCABULARY

A **Complete the conversation with your own information.**

> **A** Where are you?
>
> **B** I'm ¹ _____. And guess what?
> ² _____ is standing right next to me!
>
> **A** No way! What's ³ _____ doing?
>
> **B** ⁴ _____
>
> **A** Awesome!

B **Use the present continuous to write a conversation about a famous athlete you see. Use the words and phrases in the box or your own words. Look at the conversation in the right column and use it as a model.**

awesome	doing	guess what	score	take a photo	talk to a player
team	what	where	who	win	

A _____   **A** Where are you now?

B _____   **B** I'm at the airport. And guess what? The
                                              Giants baseball team is sitting here!

A _____   **A** Really? What are they doing?

B _____   **B** I think they're waiting for a plane.

A _____   **A** Awesome! That's your favorite team!

THE 16TH STEP

1 VOCABULARY: Exercising

A **Read the three interviews and complete the text. Use the correct form of the verbs in the box.**

> jump   lie down   lift   ~~sit down~~   stretch   throw

A Yoga is my favorite exercise. I'm waiting for my class to start. The class is very good and a lot of people take it. The teacher ¹ _____sits down_____ in front of the class and we sit behind him. Here we are ² _____ our bodies to warm up. Then we ³ _____ on the floor at the end of class. I love that part!

B My daughter is taking a dance class. She likes it because her friends from school are in the same class. The girls are ⁴ _____ their arms above their heads at the moment. The teacher asks them to follow her instructions.

C My friends and I play on a baseball team. We meet every Thursday in the park. First, we ⁵ _____ balls for a few minutes to warm up. We are ⁶ _____ up and down in the photo because we're happy! My friends and I love this sport!

2 GRAMMAR: Simple present and present continuous

A **Write the verbs in parentheses in the correct form.**

1 Tony _____plays_____ (play) football every weekend.

2 We _____ (lift) our arms at the moment.

3 Sari _____ (climb) up the stairs to get to class every day.

4 They _____ (lie) down on the floor at the moment.

5 How many people _____ (swim) in the pool right now?

6 How often _____ (he / run)?

7 What kind of exercise _____ (they / do) now?

8 _____ (your boyfriend / watch) the game on TV this afternoon?

B **Correct the sentences.**

1 Are you stretching every morning when you wake up?
_____

2 Look! I lift two coffee cups now!
_____

3 I'm not going to the gym every evening.
_____

4 Look! The fans are run onto the field!
_____

5 The race is on. Everyone is run.
_____

6 Do you listening to the game on the radio now?
_____

7 Your dog lies down under the tree.
_____

8 Are all the athletes exercise at the gym now?
_____

3 GRAMMAR AND VOCABULARY

A **Complete the gym questionnaire with your own answers.**

1 Do you exercise? _____

2 Are you a gym member? _____

3 Do you play a sport? _____

4 What is your regular exercise routine? _____

5 What sports do you like? _____

6 Do you prefer to exercise in the morning, afternoon, or at night? _____

COULD YOU TELL ME … ?

1 FUNCTIONAL LANGUAGE: Asking for information

A **Put the conversation in order.**

- [ ] Near the exit, thanks. Oh, one more thing, could you tell me where the coffee shop is?
- [ ] It's right by the entrance.
- [1] Excuse me. We're looking for row B.
- [ ] It's three rows down.
- [ ] Thank you so much and have a great day.
- [ ] They are near the exit by center court.
- [ ] Oh, great! Thanks. Do you know where the restrooms are?

B **Complete the conversation with the expressions in exercise A.**

A Excuse me. I'm [1]_____ a small sun hat for a girl.

B The sun hats are over there, on the right.

A OK, thanks. Also, [2]_____ the price of these sunglasses?

B No problem. They're $16.00.

A Oh! OK, thank you.

2 REAL-WORLD STRATEGY: Checking information

A **Match the sentences 1–5 with the correct responses a–e.**

1 Excuse me. Do you know where the VIP seats are?

2 Could you tell me when the game starts?

3 Excuse me. I'm looking for the entrance to the gym.

4 Oh wow, the score is 3–1, Manchester United.

5 Excuse me. Where is the basketball practice?

a ____ 3–1? I can't believe it!

b ____ The entrance? It's around the corner.

c ____ Basketball practice? It's at the May Center.

d ____ The game? I think it starts at 5 p.m.

e ____ The VIP seats? They are next to the court.

3 FUNCTIONAL LANGUAGE AND REAL-WORLD STRATEGY

A   **Complete the conversation. Use the words in parentheses.**

A Excuse me. ¹_____ (look for) court number three. I have a tennis lesson.

B Of course. The teacher ²_____ (wait / now). The court is out this door.

A Out this door? OK. ³_____ (could / tell) the teacher's name?

B ⁴_____? Well, it's Giuliana Silva, but we call her Ace.

A Ace? Great! Just one more thing. ⁵_____ (know / where) I can get a towel?

B ⁶_____ (towel)? Sure, no problem. I can get one for you. Here you go.

A Thank you!

B   **Use exercise A to write a similar conversation using the information below.**

BASKETBALL CLINIC

Tue–Wed 3 p.m.–9 p.m.
Main Gym
18 years old and older
Entrance – $15

A _____

B _____

A _____

B _____

A _____

B _____

A _____

BIKE SHARING

1 LISTENING

A 🔊 **3.01** **Listen to the radio interview about the *Bicitekas* in Mexico City. Read the sentences and write *T* if True or *F* if False. Write the correct answers.**

1 _____ Adrian's group has bicycle tours to teach people about art.

2 _____ Adrian rides his bicycle to his job at the theater every day.

3 _____ Adrian wears a helmet and gloves when he rides his bicycle.

4 _____ Adrian's group has night tours.

B 🔊 **3.01** **LISTEN FOR DETAIL** **Listen to the interview again and answer the questions.**

1 What is the name of Adrian's group? _____

2 Where is his group from? _____

3 How many people ride bicycles in Mexico City on the weekend? _____

4 When are the night tours? _____

5 How many people usually take the tours? _____

2 READING

A **Read the online article and (circle) the correct answers.**

Cities for People or Cars?

Too many cars can be bad for a city. There is too much traffic and stress. And traffic can be a problem because stressed drivers sometimes break the rules to save time.

At the *Bicitekas* group, we think bicycles can help change people's habits. That is why we have bicycle tours around the city, and we plan art shows and parties. Mexico City needs better roads and more green areas.

There are many ways you can help. Come to our shows, tours, and parties. And, above all, use your bike. Do not drive your car on the weekend, and share rides with friends and family. You can help us make our city a better place for people and not just for cars.

1 What is the main idea?
   a Cars are good.   b People can help.   c The city needs more parks.

2 What does *Bicitekas* do?
   a sells bicycles   b has bike tours   c repairs old bicycles

3 What does the author say people can do to help?
   a share rides   b drive on weekends   c buy a newer car

A **Match the sentences. Then complete them with the correct word from the box.**

> and   but   so

1 There aren't any bike docking stations at the subway station, _____

2 The local park has a bike lane, _____

3 My street needs a park, trees, _____

a _____ they don't rent bikes to park visitors.

b _____ more green areas.

c _____ I have to walk home from the station.

B **Use the sentences in exercise A, and write three comments on your neighborhood's website about the things missing in your area. Don't forget to use *and*, *but*, and *so*.**

CHECK AND REVIEW

Read the statements. Can you do these things?

UNIT 3	Mark the boxes. ☑ I can do it. ❓ I am not sure. I can …	If you are not sure, go back to these pages in the Student's Book.
VOCABULARY	☐ use sports words.	page 22
	☐ use words to describe exercise.	page 25
GRAMMAR	☐ use the present continuous for events happening now.	page 23
	☐ understand the difference between simple present and present continuous.	page 25
FUNCTIONAL LANGUAGE	☐ ask for information in different situations.	page 26
	☐ check information.	page 27
SKILLS	☐ write a short message.	page 29
	☐ use *and*, *but*, and *so*.	page 29

4.1 COMIC CELEBRATION

1 VOCABULARY: Describing pop culture

A **Find the words from the box in the word search.**

actor	artist	band	concert
director	festival	~~musician~~	singer
TV show	video games		

U	U	V	T	T	T	W	K	D	E	B	G
N	V	X	Q	V	T	S	D	T	F	A	C
G	I	S	V	S	Y	I	I	T	N	N	D
P	D	H	M	H	I	N	R	S	N	D	Y
L	E	R	M	O	O	G	E	I	E	N	F
V	O	S	E	W	L	E	C	T	T	A	E
K	G	B	W	G	Y	R	T	R	D	C	S
O	A	R	T	I	S	T	O	A	X	T	T
H	M	L	W	J	V	I	R	R	N	O	I
L	E	I	H	P	R	V	S	T	E	R	V
D	S	H	X	C	O	N	C	E	R	T	A
T	N	M	U	S	I	C	I	A	N	P	L

2 GRAMMAR: Present continuous for future plans

A **Label each sentence *F* for future or *P* for present.**

1 I'm going to a theater festival this weekend.   F

2 My friend's band is playing tonight at Red Note.   _____

3 She's in her room. I think she's watching a TV show.   _____

4 Are you doing anything tonight?   _____

5 I'm getting a new video game tomorrow.   _____

6 What are you listening to? Can I listen?   _____

B **Put the conversation in order.**

- [ ] I love them! What time are you leaving?
- [ ] Not really. I'm playing video games now, but that's all. How about you?
- [ ] In an hour. So, are you coming?
- [ ] Oh, yeah! I'm coming with you.
- [ ] I'm going to a music festival. A friend of mine is playing in a band.
- [ ] It's called Public Attack. The Bronxites and Sam and the Wheelers are also playing.
- [ ] That's great! What's the name of his band? Are other bands playing, too?
- [1] Are you doing anything tonight?

3 GRAMMAR AND VOCABULARY

A **Complete the chart with your own plans.**

Who	What	When
Anna	watch a movie	this weekend
Jose	go to a concert	tonight
Anna and Jose	play video games	tomorrow
I	_____	tomorrow
I	_____	this weekend
A friend and I	_____	next week

B **Write sentences using the information in exercise A.**

1 Anna is watching a movie this weekend.

2 _____

3 _____

4 _____

5 _____

6 _____

27

THE PERFECT GIFT

1 VOCABULARY: Naming gift items

A **Read the sentence about each person and then choose the best gift.**

1 Alex often works in her garden.
   a a bouquet of flowers
   b a phone charger
   c a candle
2 Jose loves his laptop.
   a candy
   b perfume
   c speakers
3 Marta always wears earrings.
   a a purse
   b jewelry
   c a phone charger

4 Jonathan always wears comfortable clothes.
   a a candle
   b a sweatshirt
   c speakers
5 Sari often eats desserts.
   a candy
   b a candle
   c perfume
6 It's really difficult to buy gifts for Tony.
   a a phone charger
   b a candle
   c a gift card

2 GRAMMAR: Object pronouns

A **Complete the sentences using the words in the box.**

her	him	it	me	them	us	you

1 I always give my mom a bouquet of flowers. It's the best gift for _____ her _____.
2 Sometimes I buy candy for my brother. It makes _____ happy!
3 Tomorrow is your birthday! I'm giving _____ speakers for your laptop.
4 My brothers, sisters, and I are going to my grandparents' house on Sunday.
   They often invite _____ for a family dinner.
5 I have a candle for you! I hope you like _____!
6 My friends know what I like. They always buy great gifts for _____!
7 I'm getting new pants for my sister. I'm buying _____ tomorrow.

B **Rewrite the sentences using object pronouns.**

1 Donald is a Yankees' baseball fan. He watches **the Yankees** play every weekend.

   Donald is a Yankees' baseball fan. He watches them play every weekend.

2 I'm buying a new camera for you. I hope you like **the new camera**.

   _____

3 Those are beautiful flowers! Do you like **the flowers**?

   _____

4 My dad always gives me good advice. I love **my dad**!

   _____

5 Jack, Katie, and I are going to Comic Con. I'm glad you're coming with **Jack, Katie, and me**.

   _____

6 It's my sister's birthday. She has so many hobbies, I don't know what to give **my sister**.

   _____

3 GRAMMAR AND VOCABULARY

A **Complete the conversation with your own information.**

A I want to give my ¹_____ a birthday gift, but I don't know what to get ²_____.

B OK, well. What does ³_____ like to do? What are ⁴_____ hobbies?

A I'm not sure. I think ⁵_____ likes ⁶_____.

B OK. How about ⁷_____? Do you think ⁸_____ might like ⁹_____?

A That's a great idea! Thanks for helping ¹⁰_____!

B Sure! That's what friends are for!

4.3 I'D LOVE TO!

1 FUNCTIONAL LANGUAGE: Making and responding to invitations; making plans to meet

A   **Match the columns to complete the conversations.**

1   Would you like to come to the concert tonight?   a _____ Great! See you there!
2   We can meet you at seven at the theater.   b _____ Not much. How about you?
3   Let's meet in front of the bus station.   c _____ OK, let's meet there at seven.
4   Hey, Ray! What's up?   d _____ OK. Where is the station from here?
5   We're meeting at the entrance to the park.   e _____ Sorry, I can't. I'm busy tonight.

2 REAL-WORLD STRATEGY: Giving general excuses

A   **Complete the chart with sentences from the conversation.**

1   **A**   Hi, Lauren. Mark and I are going dancing. Would you like to come?
2   **B**   I'm not sure. I have homework and everything.
3   **A**   Come with us! We can leave in two hours. Can you finish your homework in two hours?
4   **B**   I think I can. OK, I'd love to.
5   **A**   Great! We can meet at my place in two hours. We're getting a taxi from there.
6   **B**   OK. See you there!

Purpose	Number of line
Decide on a time and a place to meet	_____
Say yes to the invitation	_____
Say no and give a general excuse	_____
Invite someone to do something with you	1
Agree on your new plans	_____
Explain more about the plans	_____

3 FUNCTIONAL LANGUAGE AND REAL-WORLD STRATEGY

A **Look at the pictures and choose one event. You will write a conversation planning to meet with friends at this event.**

B **Before you write the conversation, complete the chart with expressions you plan to use.**

Purpose	Expressions
Ask how people are	What's up?
Ask about their plans	What are you doing …?
Invite someone to do something with you	
Give a general excuse	
Explain more about the plans	
Accept the invitation	
Decide on a time and a place to meet	
Agree on your new plans	

C **Write your conversation with the expressions from exercise B.**

A Hey. _____?

B _____

A _____

B _____

A _____

B _____

A _____

B _____

A _____

4.4 WAITING FOR SOMETHING SPECIAL

1 LISTENING

A 🔊 **4.01** Listen to the podcast. (Circle) the correct answers.

1 What is the name of the festival?

  a The Black Rock City Festival   **b** Burning Man   **c** The Nevada Festival

2 What is the festival famous for?

  a its people   **b** its fans   **c** its art

3 How long does it last?

  a a year   **b** a week   **c** a month

4 The festival happens in _____ .

  a the city   **b** the jungle   **c** the desert

B 🔊 **4.01** **LISTEN FOR DETAIL** Listen to the podcast again. Match the phrases to complete the sentences.

1	This year about 70,000 people …	**a** _____	help you find the artist in you.
2	It is a time for them …	**b** _____	TV shows talk about it.
3	They say it can …	**c** _____	for a whole week.
4	People live in the desert …	**d** _____	are coming to Nevada.
5	It is so popular that …	**e** _____	to meet other people.
6	This is the thirty-third year …	**f** _____	of the festival.

2 READING

A **Read the blog post and (circle) the correct answers.**

My Day at Burning Man

So I get up in the morning, I brush my teeth, and I see a plate with cheese sandwiches at my door. I eat **them** – they taste great! I get dressed, ride my bike around my village, and I find a small airplane. I get on the plane and fly with a man named Rick for 30 minutes. I can see the whole desert city from above – **it** is so great!

5   After my plane ride, I'm getting hungry. So, I ride my bike again and find a vegetarian stand, because I don't eat meat. I get a carrot milkshake and a veggie burger, and I'm ready to go again. I see a pink car, a white table, and lots of balloons in the sky. I join a Shakespeare theater group and play the part of Hamlet. The lines are difficult, but I read **them** anyway. It's getting dark now, so **we** all go to a Daft Punk concert near the wooden Burning Man.

10   That's a normal day at the Burning Man festival in Black Rock City. I love **it** here!

1	The word *them* in line 2 means _____ .	**a** teeth	**b** tents	**c** sandwiches
2	The word *it* in line 4 means _____ .	**a** an airplane	**b** a bike	**c** a city
3	The word *them* in line 8 means _____ .	**a** a theater group	**b** lines in a play	**c** balloons
4	The word *we* in line 9 means _____ .	**a** the band	**b** a theater group	**c** Rick and his friends
5	The word *it* in line 10 means _____ .	**a** a wooden man	**b** a festival	**c** a concert

3 WRITING

A 🔊 **4.01** Listen to the podcast again and read the information below. Write an email and invite your friend to the Burning Man festival. Use the information below to write your invitation. Check your spelling.

DATE: **August 27 – September 4**

PRICE: **$425.00**

EVENTS: **Theater groups, Fire circles, Music concerts, Art competition**

PLACE: **Black Rock City in the Nevada desert**

Reply   Forward

To: _____

Subject: Burning Man Festival

Hi!

CHECK AND REVIEW

Read the statements. Can you do these things?

UNIT 4

Mark the boxes. ☑ I can do it. ? I am not sure. I can ...		If you are not sure, go back to these pages in the Student's Book.
VOCABULARY	☐ use words to talk about pop culture.	page 34
	☐ use words to talk about gifts.	page 36
GRAMMAR	☐ use the present continuous to talk about future plans.	page 35
	☐ use object pronouns.	page 37
FUNCTIONAL LANGUAGE	☐ make and respond to invitations.	page 38
	☐ make plans to meet.	page 38
	☐ use general language to give excuses.	page 39
SKILLS	☐ write an online invitation.	page 41

1   VOCABULARY: Describing opinions and feelings

A   **Look at the emojis and label them using the words in the box.**

amazing	angry	cool	crazy	~~dangerous~~	fun
horrible	loud	perfect	proud	strange	tired

1 _____

2 _____

3 _____

4 _____

5 _____

6 _____

7   *dangerous*

8 _____

9 _____

10 _____

11 _____

12 _____

2   GRAMMAR: Simple past

A   **Read the clues and complete the crossword with the past form of the verbs in bold.**

Across:

2   They **are** my friends.

3   I **have** a lot of work to do.

6   It **is** my birthday.

7   I **study** for my test in the library.

8   What **do** you do for fun?

Down:

1   I **learn** new things in art class.

2   Tim **walks** five miles to school.

4   I often **visit** the aquarium in Boston.

5   The cat **rests** in the sun all afternoon.

6   I **go** to work early in the morning.

B **Rewrite the sentences using the past form of the verbs and the words in parentheses.**

1 I see my friends at school every day. (yesterday)

_____

2 They visit their grandparents every year. (last year)

_____

3 Is he your best friend? (in elementary school)

_____

4 Sam has dinner plans with her classmates. (last night)

_____

5 Are the Patriots the winners this season? (last season)

_____

3 GRAMMAR AND VOCABULARY

A **Write three short stories about your past that were:**

Amazing: _____

_____

_____

Dangerous: _____

_____

_____

Strange: _____

_____

_____

B **Choose two stories from exercise A and answer the following questions about them.**

Questions	First story	Second story
Was this good or bad for you?		
Who were you with?		
Why was this moment special?		

5.2 GUESS IN 60 SECONDS

1 VOCABULARY: Describing life events

A **Write each action under the correct life stage.**

be born	become a grandparent	buy a car
~~buy a house or apartment~~	get a job	get married
graduate from college	have a baby	learn to drive
meet your future husband/wife	retire	start school

Children and youth	Adults	Old age
	buy a house or apartment	

2 GRAMMAR: Simple past negative and questions

A **Put the words in the correct order to make sentences.**

1 move / Mia / When / to / did / Rio de Janeiro?

   When did Mia move to Rio de Janeiro?

2 did / go / Mia / school / to / Where?

3 brother's / her / name / was / What?

4 meet / her / she / husband / did / Where?

5 and her husband / children / did / have / How many / Mia?

6 children / didn't / have / They / three.

7 her / job / was / What?

8 did / How long / she / there / work?

9 Did / her / job / like / she?

10 Did / her / his / husband / job / like?

B Complete the interview about a famous Brazilian soccer player, Pelé. Use the past forms of the words in the box. Some words will be used more than once.

be	become	do	help
(not) be	play	score	

When ¹_____was_____ Pelé born?

He was born on October 23, 1940.

Where ²_____ he born?

In Três Corações, Brazil.

What ³_____ his life like?

Pelé ⁴_____ rich when he was born. He grew up very poor, but he was always a great soccer player.
He ⁵_____ a professional soccer player when he ⁶_____ 15 years old. One year later, he ⁷_____ more goals than any other player and ⁸_____ for Brazil's national team.

When ⁹_____ he become a superstar?

At the 1958 World Cup in Sweden. At 17 years old, he ¹⁰_____ three goals in the semifinal against France, and ¹¹_____ the Brazilian team become the world's best team when they scored two more goals in the final game against Sweden.

3 GRAMMAR AND VOCABULARY

A Look at Pelé's personal fact file and write sentences about him.

First marriage	Rosemeri dos Reis Cholbi, February 21, 1966
First baby	Kelly Cristina, January 1967
First grandchild	August 1987
College	No
First World Cup	1958, 17 years old
Last World Cup	Mexico 1970
Retirement	1977
FIFA Ballon d'Or Prix d'Honneur	January 2014

Personal life

Pelé married Rosemeri dos Reis Cholbi on February 21, 1966.

_____

_____

World Cup victories

_____

_____

Age when he retired, and what he did after that

_____

_____

5.3 THAT'S COOL!

1 FUNCTIONAL LANGUAGE: Congratulating and sympathizing with people

A   **(Circle)** the best expression to complete the conversations.

1 You got the job!

    a You did really well!   **b** Congratulations!   **c** Never mind.

2 I passed the test.

    a I'm so sorry!   **b** Never mind.   **c** That's great news!

3 She lost her keys.

    a I'm so sorry.   **b** Congratulations!   **c** That's great news!

4 She spent ten hours in the airport.

    a Never mind.   **b** That's terrible. Talk about bad luck.   **c** Don't worry about it.

5 I forgot your books.

    a Great job!   **b** That's terrible. Talk about bad luck.   **c** Don't worry about it.

2 REAL-WORLD STRATEGY: Checking your understanding

A   **Match each statement to the best response.**

1 I thought you said his house was near.

2 We have a new member of the family!

3 I'm a writer!

4 I'm disappointed!

5 So you mean it's not safe to swim in the ocean?

a _____ You mean you published your novel?

b _____ So you mean you didn't win first prize?

c _____ I meant it's not safe now, but maybe you can swim later.

d _1_ I meant it's near my house, not yours.

e _____ Do you mean you had a baby?

3 FUNCTIONAL LANGUAGE AND REAL-WORLD STRATEGY

A **Complete the conversation with the best expressions.**

A I heard you got married last month! ¹_____!

B We did! Thanks! It was a really big decision.

A ²_____ it was a life decision?

B Yes! I'm really happy about it! We went to Rio after the wedding.

A ³_____!

B I know! Jim and I were really busy the month before!

A I'm sure you were. ⁴_____!

B Thanks!

B **Look at the picture. Write a conversation between the two friends using the correct sympathy expressions. Use the conversation in exercise A as a model.**

A Hey, I heard you had an accident.

B ¹_____.

A ²_____ Did you get hurt?

B Yes, well, I went to the hospital. But I'm OK now.

A ³_____.

B Thanks! ⁴_____.

5.4 FIRST IMPRESSIONS

1 LISTENING

A 🔊 **5.01** **LISTEN FOR DETAIL** Listen to the story and (circle) the correct answers. Then listen again to check your answers.

1 Why did Philippe want to go to the Caribbean?

   a He wanted to teach French.

   b He never visited before.

   c He wanted to see his family.

2 Where is Claire from?

   a Anse Noire   b Bogotá   c Martinique

3 How did Claire feel after going fishing?

   a excited   b proud   c perfect

4 What problem did Claire have on her vacation?

   a She didn't speak French.   b She didn't like the food.   c She didn't know anyone there.

5 What does Claire want to do before she returns to Martinique?

   a take swimming lessons   b learn to cook   c study French

2 READING

A **READING FOR MAIN IDEAS** Read the text. Then (circle) the correct words to complete the sentences.

My first time in Buenos Aires was amazing and strange at the same time. I'm from a small town in Oklahoma, so I like quiet and food – lots of food. And I had lots of great meals in Buenos Aires, especially the meat.

Everything was great for the first two days, but it changed on the third day. This happened when the town's soccer team, *River Plate*, won the *Libertadores* Cup for the fifth time.

That evening, soccer fans partied all night in the streets. There was loud music and dancing everywhere! I was not able to sleep! I don't understand why people do that when their team wins.

All this taught me a lesson. I love Buenos Aires – the people, the food – I even love Argentinian soccer! So, I want to go back, but not during any big soccer games. That I'm sure of.

1 The text is about *soccer fans in / a trip to* Buenos Aires.

2 The writer *liked / didn't like* Argentinian food.

3 The writer enjoyed *all of his time / part of his time* in Buenos Aires.

4 He learned never to travel to Argentina *again / during soccer games*.

B Read the text again and answer the questions below.

1 What's the name of the Buenos Aires soccer team? _____

2 Where in the US is the writer from? _____

3 What food did he eat a lot in Buenos Aires? _____

4 Does the writer love Argentinian soccer? _____

5 Is he ever going back to Buenos Aires? _____

A   **Read the conversations. Complete them with the phrases in the box. Some phrases can be used more than once.**

> Absolutely!   Are you kidding?   I know the feeling.   Interesting!
> No way!   You're so right.

1 **A** I had a great time in Seattle! What about you?

   B ___Absolutely!___ We had so much fun there!

2 **A** Was it difficult for you to order food in Bogotá?

   B _____ We ate anything we wanted, and people in the restaurants were always friendly.

3 **A** When I got to Berlin, I didn't understand German at all!

   B _____ I was there last year, and the same thing happened to me.

4 **A** Wow. There were a lot of police officers in American airports!

   B _____ I had the same experience.

5 **A** Paris is a very unfriendly place!

   B _____ I think it's a very friendly city.

6 **A** People in Hawaii traditionally say "Aloha" and give you a beautiful flower when you first arrive.

   B _____

7 **A** I was so tired when I arrived in Sydney.

   B _____ I slept for ten hours when I went to Hong Kong.

8 **A** Do you want to live and work in another country?

   B _____ I love living here!

CHECK AND REVIEW

Read the statements. Can you do these things?

UNIT 5	Mark the boxes. ☑ I can do it. ? I am not sure. I can …	If you are not sure, go back to these pages in the Student's Book.
VOCABULARY	☐ use adjectives to describe opinions and feelings.	page 44
	☐ use words to describe life events.	page 46
GRAMMAR	☐ use the simple past to talk about past experiences.	page 45
	☐ use the simple past negative to ask and answer questions about the past.	page 47
FUNCTIONAL LANGUAGE	☐ congratulate and sympathize with people.	page 48
	☐ check my understanding.	page 49
SKILLS	☐ write responses to comments about experiences.	page 51
	☐ agree and disagree.	page 51

1   VOCABULARY: Using money

A   **Complete the sentences with the correct form of the verbs in the box.**

borrow	cost	lend	save
~~sell~~	shop online	spend	waste

1   That store is _____selling_____ TVs at a very good price. They _____ very little money.
My brother asked me to _____ him some money so he can buy one. I want to get one, too!

2   I _____ money from Davon to buy a few video games on Black Friday. But that day, I
_____ a lot of money. I need to save money now!

3   Yes, ma'am you can buy two sweaters for the price of one and _____ half on the final price.

4   My wife likes to _____ – she loves the internet! She bought two dresses online, but they
were too small. That was a _____ of time!

2   GRAMMAR: *be going to*

A   **Put the words in the correct order to make sentences and questions.**

1   new / order / to / I'm / the / going / video game.
I'm going to order the new video game.

2   sell / going / Cara / is / her / to / car.

3   pay / to / you / me / Are / going / back?

4   all that / to / spend / going / Is / she / money?

5   aren't / they / going / to / money / No, / waste / on that.

6   bank / going / me / lend / The / isn't / to / the money.

B   **Look at the to-do list. Then write sentences.**

4G	12:00	
To-do list		
Saturday:	**Sunday:**	**Questions:**
[x] **Don:** buy new jacket	[x] **Dave:** borrow Kim's car	**Dave:** work on weekend?
[✓] **Mila:** take French class	[x] **Cal:** go to Boston	**Mila:** buy Cal a gift? this week
[✓] **Me:** order a book online	[✓] **Me and Cal:** spend time together	**Ann:** go running? Friday
[✓] **Don and Cal:** pay Jon back		

1   Don isn't going to buy a new jacket on Saturday.
2   Mila _____
3   I _____
4   Don and Cal _____
5   Dave _____
6   Cal _____
7   Cal and I _____
8   _____ Dave _____ ?
9   _____ Mila _____ ?
10 _____ Ann _____ ?

3   GRAMMAR AND VOCABULARY

A   **What are you doing this weekend? Use the words in the box and *be going to* to write sentences and questions about your weekend. Give information about who, what, when, and where.**

borrow	buy	go to	~~lend~~	order
pay back	sell	spend money on	spend time with	~~work on~~

1   My brother and I are going to work on my motorcycle on Saturday.
2   _____
3   _____
4   _____
5   _____
6   _____
7   _____
8   Is Tony going to lend me his laptop on Friday?
9   _____ ?
10 _____ ?

6.2 SHOP THIS WAY

1 VOCABULARY: Shopping

A **Write each word in the correct category.**

cart	cash register	~~customer~~	department store	drugstore
grocery store	price	sale	sales clerk	shelf

People	Places	Things
customer		

2 GRAMMAR: Determiners

A **Complete the sentences using the determiners in the box.**

all	~~all of~~	many	most	none	some

1 _____All of_____ the stores in town have great prices today.
2 _____ of the customers prefer shopping online – three out of five people say they prefer it.
3 _____ of us like to waste time waiting in line.
4 _____ of them bought new clothes on Friday. They are all very happy.
5 You can save _____ money when the store has a sale.
6 _____ malls are open tonight until midnight. Only one closed early.

B **Correct the sentences.**

1 All department stores in the city have sales.
   All of the department stores in the city have sales.
2 No customers who shop here like the long lines at the cash registers.
   _____
3 Most them are going to borrow money from the bank.
   _____
4 Some of malls are going to offer better discounts.
   _____
5 None sales clerks are very friendly today.
   _____
6 Many the sales signs in this store have the wrong information.
   _____

3 GRAMMAR AND VOCABULARY

A   Imagine you are the manager of a grocery store. You want to know what your customers think about your store. Complete the questions to ask customers about shopping there. Use the determiners, words, and phrases in the boxes.

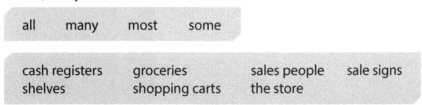

all	many	most	some

cash registers	groceries	sales people	sale signs
shelves	shopping carts	the store	

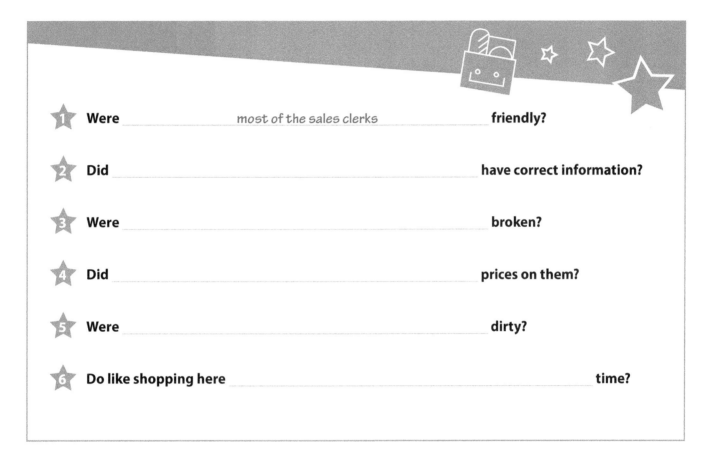

1   **Were** _____ *most of the sales clerks* _____ **friendly?**

2   **Did** _____ **have correct information?**

3   **Were** _____ **broken?**

4   **Did** _____ **prices on them?**

5   **Were** _____ **dirty?**

6   **Do like shopping here** _____ **time?**

B   Complete the following sentences with your own answers.

1   Most of the department stores in my town _____

2   None of the department stores in my town _____

3   All of the grocery stores in my town _____

4   Some of the malls in my town _____

5   Many stores in my town _____

WHAT DO YOU CALL THEM IN ENGLISH?

1 FUNCTIONAL LANGUAGE: Phrases to use when you don't know the word

A **Complete the conversation with the words in the box.**

call	~~know~~	like	thing	use

A Hi. Can I help you?

B Yes, please. I'm looking for … I don't ¹_____know_____ the word in English. It's a ²_____ to connect electronics.

A Hmm … You mean an "adapter"?

B Not exactly. It's ³_____ an adapter, but you ⁴_____ it to plug in a lot of devices at once.

A Oh, got it! We do have them. Power strips.

B What do you ⁵_____ them in English?

A Power strips.

B That's right! Thanks!

2 REAL-WORLD STRATEGY: Asking for words in English

A **Read the conversation. Complete it with the correct expressions.**

A Hi, do you need any help?

B Hi, yes. I'm looking for some things. You use them to eat. How do ¹_____?

A I'm not sure. You mean like spoons?

B No. They're like spoons, but you use them to cut food. What's ²_____ for them?

A Knives.

B What ³_____ again?

A Knives.

B That's right, thank you.

3 FUNCTIONAL LANGUAGE AND REAL-WORLD STRATEGY

A   You're going to write a conversation. First, look at the pictures below. Find out what the items are called in English – use your dictionary or go online. Write the words under the pictures. Then follow the instructions in exercise B.

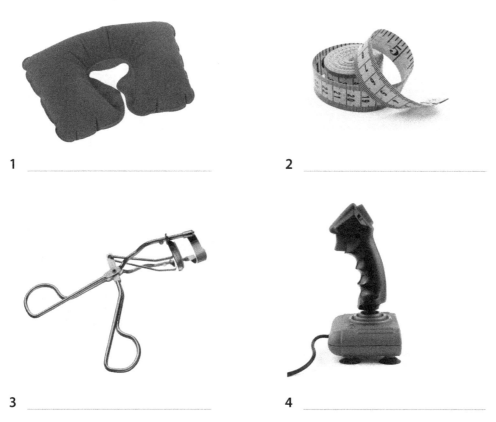

1 _____

2 _____

3 _____

4 _____

B   Before you write the conversation, complete the chart with expressions you plan to use.

Offering to help	
Explaining your language problem	
Explaining the function of the thing you want	
Asking the name in English	
Saying you understand	

C   Write your conversation with the expressions from exercise B.

A   Hi. _____ ?

B   Yes, please. I'm looking for … I _____ .
    It's _____ .

A   What is it for?

B   You _____ .

A   Ah! I _____ ! _____ .

B   What _____ ?

A   _____ .

B   That's right. Thanks!

MONEY LESSONS

1 LISTENING

A 🔊 **6.01** Listen to the radio program. (Circle) the correct words to complete the sentences.

1 The program is about *street markets / smart shopping*.

2 The speaker thinks shopping lists *are / aren't* a good idea.

3 It *is / is not* a good idea to pay with credit cards.

4 It's a good idea to *never / always* save every time you shop.

B 🔊 **6.01** **LISTEN FOR DETAIL** Listen to the radio program again. Match the phrases to the correct topic.

1 Know how much you want to spend.   a _____ Use cash.

2 Credit cards are dangerous.   b _____ Save first, spend later.

3 Put a little in the bank.   c _____ Make a list.

4 You lose nothing when you ask.   d _1_ Decide a number.

5 Write down what you need and want.   e _____ Discuss the price.

2 READING

A **Read the blog post. Choose the correct answers below.**

> My trip to Rio is going to be amazing! I can't wait to go shopping there! Brazilians dress well, so I always check what's in their stores.
>
> Gilson Martins is a large store in Rio. Sometimes international movie stars shop there! Now, be careful because, as Brazilians say: *A única coisa fácil sobre o dinheiro e perdê-lo*. It means that the only easy thing about money is losing it. Prices in this store are high, and you can spend lots of money in just one visit.
>
> Perhaps my favorite shopping trip was on my last visit there. I went to the street markets in Ipanema. I found nice leather bags and beautiful pictures. I was careful with what I bought because Brazilians also say: *O barato sai caro*: Cheap things can be very expensive.
>
> I am going to have so much fun shopping! But I also plan not to spend a lot because: *Dinheiro não dá em árvores*. Money doesn't grow on trees!

1 What kind of blog is this?

   a a travel blog   b a work blog   c a business blog

2 What does the writer enjoy in Rio?

   a movie stars   b fashion   c shopping

3 Why does the writer say that cheap things from street markets can be expensive?

   a Because they aren't always very good.   b Because you can buy them only in Brazil.

   c Because you can't return them.

4 Why does the writer say that money doesn't grow on trees?

   a Money is hard to get, so don't waste it.   b Money is hard to find in Brazil.

   c Shopping is difficult work.

WRITING

A **Rewrite the sentences using *one / ones* and *it*.**

1 Movie stars are the <u>famous people</u> that shop there.

_____

2 Ipanema's street market is great. I can't wait to visit <u>my favorite market</u> again.

_____

3 There are many stores in Rio. Gilson Martins is a famous <u>store</u>.

_____

4 Of all the countries, Brazil is the <u>country</u> I'm in love with.

_____

5 Brazilians are the <u>people</u> that dress well.

_____

B **Here is something else Brazilians say: *Quanto mais se tem, mais se quer.* It means: The more you have, the more you want. Write a vlog script explaining the meaning of this saying in English. When would you use this saying? Use *ones* and *it*.**

CHECK AND REVIEW

Read the statements. Can you do these things?

UNIT 6	Mark the boxes. ☑ I can do it. ? I am not sure. I can …		If you are not sure, go back to these pages in the Student's Book.
VOCABULARY	☐ use money words.		page 54
	☐ use shopping words.		page 56
GRAMMAR	☐ use *be going to* to talk about future plans.		page 55
	☐ use determiners to talk about quantity.		page 57
FUNCTIONAL LANGUAGE	☐ use phrases to say what I want when I don't know the word.		page 58
	☐ ask how to say something in English.		page 59
SKILLS	☐ write a vlog script.		page 61
	☐ use *it* and *ones*.		page 61

7.1 COMFORT FOOD

1 VOCABULARY: Naming food

A Look at the pictures and complete the crossword.

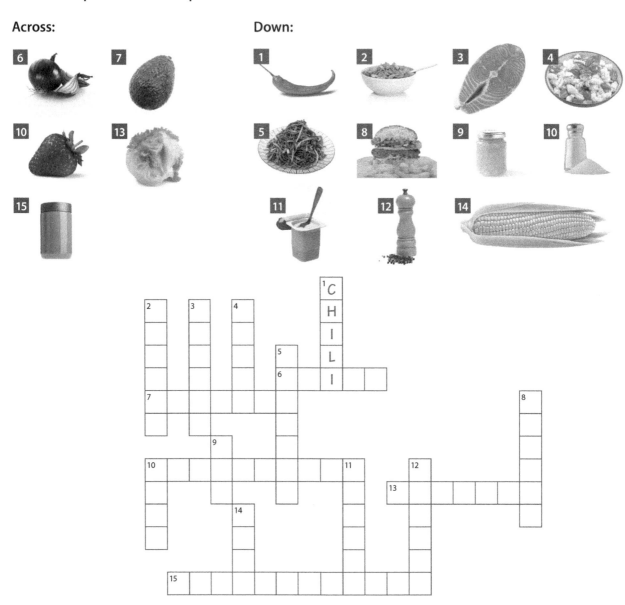

Across:

6   7   10   13   15

Down:

1   2   3   4   5   8   9   10   11   12   14

2 GRAMMAR: Quantifiers

A Circle the correct words to complete the questions.
1 How *much* / *many* bowls of cereal and how *much* / *many* fruit do you eat every day?
2 How *much* / *many* burgers and how *much* / *many* salmon do you eat each week?
3 How *much* / *many* salt and pepper do you add to your food?
4 How *much* / *many* pasta and how *much* / *many* chilies do you eat in a week?

B **Correct the sentences using the words in the box.**

> a little   a lot   many   much   some

1 I'm putting many of onion in my salad.

   I'm putting a lot of onion in my salad.

2 You just need a few blueberry jam to add flavor.

   _____

3 I'm adding a few yogurt to my bowl of fruit.

   _____

4 There are too much noodles to put them all in one bowl.

   _____

5 We added too many salt to our dinner.

   _____

6 Let's add a few more pepper to the pasta.

   _____

3 GRAMMAR AND VOCABULARY

A **Complete the conversation below with your own information.**

A Do you remember your favorite comfort food when you were a kid?

B Yes, I do. It was ¹_____.

A And how *much / many* ²_____ did you eat in a week?

B I think I ate *a lot of / some / a few / a little* ³_____ every week.

A What did you like to eat it with?

B I loved to eat it with ⁴_____.

A How *much / many* ⁵_____ do you eat now?

B I eat *a lot / some / a few / a little*.

A What's your favorite comfort food now?

B It's ⁶_____, but I also eat *a lot of / some / a few / a little* ⁷_____ every week.

51

7.2 EAT IN THE STREET

1 VOCABULARY: Describing food

A **Complete the sentences with the words in the box.**

bitter	~~boiled~~	delicious	fresh	fried
grilled	raw	roasted	sour	spicy

1 I hate _____*boiled*_____ eggs in my salad!
2 This lemon is too _____ for me.
3 I prefer a _____ salad for lunch.
4 Those chilies are very _____, but I don't mind hot foods.
5 In some Japanese foods, the fish is _____. They don't cook it.
6 I usually don't add sugar to my coffee, but this one is too _____!
7 The meat comes with _____ onions and peppers. Everything is cooked at the same time.
8 Thanks for cooking dinner. It was really _____! Is there more?
9 I planned on making _____ chicken for dinner tomorrow, but my oven is not working.
10 Are you having some _____ potatoes with your burger?

2 GRAMMAR: Verb patterns

A **Put the words in the correct order to make sentences.**

1 for / I / stand / my / waiting / can't / food.
   I can't stand waiting for my food.
2 food truck / the / ordering / love / from / We / on the corner.
   _____
3 than to / cook / prefers to / dinner / Ali / go out.
   _____
4 mind / in / I / waiting / don't / line.
   _____
5 own / cooking / you / like / your / Do / meals?
   _____
6 order / like / the / to / would / He / grilled salmon.
   _____
7 eating / Do / enjoy / you / spicy food?
   _____
8 hate / We / the dishes / doing / after dinner.
   _____
9 want / Do / eat out / they / to / on Friday night?
   _____

52

B **Circle the correct words to complete the sentences.**

1 My best friend loves _____ Indian food.

   a eat   **b** to eat   **c** ate

2 Claire would like _____ for us tonight.

   a to cook   **b** cooking   **c** cook

3 Do you want _____ dessert as well?

   a ordering   **b** ordered   **c** to order

4 I _____ waiting a few more minutes.

   a don't mind   **b** want   **c** woud like

5 She _____ to add spicy sauce to her Mexican food.

   a enjoys   **b** can't stand   **c** loves

6 I want _____ you out for dinner tomorrow. Are you free?

   a to take   **b** taking   **c** take

3 GRAMMAR AND VOCABULARY

A **Think about a food truck or restaurant you know. Write some opinions for their comments page. Use the words in the box for ideas.**

delicious	eat raw food	fried	have fresh food
have more sauce options	have the same food	order online	~~try new food~~
types of sauce	wait for the check	wait to order	

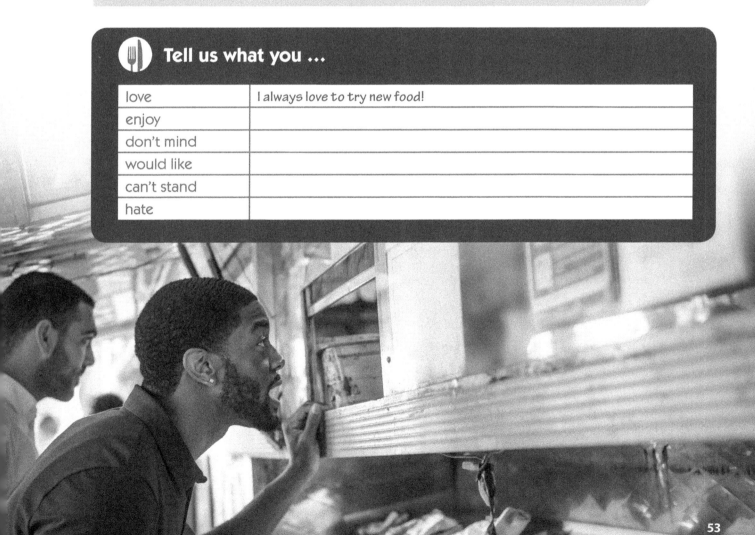

Tell us what you …

love	I always love to try new food!
enjoy	
don't mind	
would like	
can't stand	
hate	

I'LL HAVE THE CHICKEN

1 FUNCTIONAL LANGUAGE: Ordering food and taking food orders

A **Put the conversation in order.**

☐ Oh, I'm allergic to nuts.

☐ Perfect! I'll be right back.

☐ It comes with avocado, tomatoes, potatoes, peanuts, and the house dressing.

☐ Well, today's special is the chicken salad.

☐ Oh, OK. No nuts. Anything to drink?

☐ OK, we can add almonds instead.

☐1 Hi, are you ready to order?

☐ I mean, I'm allergic to <u>all</u> kinds of nuts.

☐ What does it come with?

☐ I'll have a soda.

☐ Yes, what do you recommend?

2 REAL-WORLD STRATEGY: *I mean*

A **Complete the conversations with the correct expressions.**

B Excuse me? What ¹ ___comes with___ the burger?

A It comes with lettuce, tomato, and avocado.

B ² _____, do French fries come with it?

A You can have French fries and a drink for two dollars more.

B Oh, OK. ³ _____ just a burger, please.

A How was the food?

B It was very good, thanks.

A ⁴ _____ some dessert?

B Not today, thanks. ⁵ _____?

A Sure. Here you go.

3 FUNCTIONAL LANGUAGE AND REAL-WORLD STRATEGY

A   Read the situations in the chart. Write the correct response to the questions and suggestions.

	Server	You
You are allergic to milk.	"The chef says there is some yogurt in the dressing."	I mean, I can't have any milk at all.
You are on a diet.	"Can I get you a dessert?"	
You are vegetarian.	"The soup is made with chicken, rice, and vegetables."	
You want to order dessert.	"Would you like anything else?"	
You ordered the grilled salmon.	"Here's your order, fried fish with grilled vegetables."	

B   Choose one of the situations about diets in exercise A. Think of an idea for a food truck that sells food for people with this special diet. Complete the chart below with the information about your food truck.

The name of your food truck:	
Who your customers are:	
Specials and how they are cooked:	
The price of your food:	

IMPOSSIBLE FOODS

1 LISTENING

A 🔊 **7.01** **Listen to the radio interviews. Number the speakers in the order you hear them.**

☐ Keila Summers, regular customer at The Origins restaurant

☐ Melissa Poitras, vegetarian and animal lover

☐ Charles Davis, chef at The Origins restaurant

☐ Carol Saint Vincent, restaurant writer

The Origins restaurant invites you to a special event

Be the first to try our **MEAT-FREE BURGER**

Thursday March 27

B 🔊 **7.01** **LISTEN FOR DETAIL** **Listen to the radio interviews again. Match the speakers with their opinions.**

1 Carol Saint Vincent   a ____ "I think this is a delicious burger …"

2 Charles Davis   b ____ "But mostly it tasted like some strange meat …"

3 Keila Summers   c ____ "For me, it tasted amazing …"

4 Melissa Poitras   d ____ "I'm so happy to write about this delicious burger."

2 READING

A **Read the food blog below. Then circle the correct answers.**

Burgers that taste like meat, but have no meat in them, are an amazing idea. Of course, they're also good for the health of both people and the planet. But most of us don't change our eating habits for food that tastes the same. It has to taste better! For example, some people in New York love the Best Burger, made by Dave Simmons, a popular chef. His grilled burger is made of cereal and mushrooms. It doesn't taste like meat, but it is really delicious. What do you think? Is the future of food all about science, or is it about what the customer wants?

1 The writer thinks that burgers with no meat are ____

   a the future of food   b a bad habit   c a great idea

2 The writer thinks that burgers without meat need to ____

   a be more popular than meat   b taste better than meat   c taste like meat

3 The Best Burger is ____

   a raw   b grilled   c fresh

4 What is the Best Burger mostly made of?

   a salmon   b meat   c mushrooms

3 WRITING

A **Complete the interview. Use the expressions in the box.**

> for me   my point of view   think   you ask me

Professor, you were the first person to make a "no-meat" burger in a science center. What do you think is the next step?

"From [1]_____ , it's all about helping the planet. A few months ago, someone asked me: 'Can you do this with chicken?' If [2]_____ , that is an interesting idea. I [3]_____ there are always many ways to find answers to a problem: for example, people can just eat less chicken, but we know they will not. [4]_____ , what is important is to answer a real problem, not to make new foods for the market."

B **Read the professor's opinion again. Do you agree or disagree with his comments? Why? What is your idea to help the planet? Write a blog post and explain your point of view.**

CHECK AND REVIEW

Read the statements. Can you do these things?

UNIT 7	Mark the boxes. ☑ I can do it. ⃞? I am not sure. I can …	If you are not sure, go back to these pages in the Student's Book.
VOCABULARY	⃞ use food vocabulary.	page 66
	⃞ use words to describe food.	page 68
GRAMMAR	⃞ use quantifiers to talk about amounts.	page 67
	⃞ use verb patterns to say what I like.	page 69
FUNCTIONAL LANGUAGE	⃞ order food and take food orders.	page 70
	⃞ use *I mean* to give more details.	page 71
SKILLS	⃞ write a comment about an online article.	page 73
	⃞ give my opinion.	page 73

8.1   HOME – HERE AND THERE

1   VOCABULARY: Traveling

A   **~~Cross out~~ the word that is different.**

1	tourists	tour guide	~~check-in counter~~
2	backpack	luggage	tour bus
3	backpack	check-in counter	suitcase
4	bus station	flight details	airplane
5	guidebooks	maps	tour guide

2   GRAMMAR: *if* and *when*

A   **Match the two halves of the sentences.**

1	When I stay in hotels, …	**a**	_____	I find the check-in counter first.
2	When I only have one suitcase, …	**b**	_____	I always bring a map to know where I am.
3	When I arrive at the airport, …	**c**	_____	I always sleep late.
4	When we take a tour bus, …	**d**	_____	we always see a lot of the city.
5	If I'm in a city for the first time, …	**e**	_____	I don't usually check my luggage.

B Use the information in the chart to write complete sentences.

If / When	Situation	Option
When	Kim travels to Hawaii	stay near the beach
If	Matt flies internationally	travel first class
When	we visit a new town	try the food
If	they plan a trip	use guidebooks to get ideas
When	I go on a bus tour	bring my camera with me

1 _____
2 _____
3 _____
4 _____
5 _____

3 GRAMMAR AND VOCABULARY

A Use the information in the chart to write questions using *if* or *when*.

Situation	Option 1	Option 2
travel abroad	bring one suitcase	bring more than one suitcase
have free time	visit new places	do nothing and stay home
go sightseeing	bring a guidebook	bring a map
go hiking	travel with a suitcase	travel with a backpack
go on vacation	meet new people	spend time with friends

1 When you travel abroad, do you bring one suitcase or more than one suitcase?
2 _____
3 _____
4 _____
5 _____

B Answer the questions in exercise A with your own information.

1 _____
2 _____
3 _____
4 _____
5 _____

TICKET TO RIDE

1 VOCABULARY: Using transportation

A **Find the words from the box in the word search.**

catch	change	drop off	get into
get off	get on	~~get out of~~	miss
pick up	take		

2 GRAMMAR: Giving reasons using *to* and *for*

A **Circle the correct answers to complete the sentences.**

1 Lauren is changing trains *for* / *to* get to her office.
2 We are stopping at the next town *for* / *to* breakfast.
3 I'm going into the bus station *for* / *to* buy a ticket.
4 They took a different flight *for* / *to* spend more time in San Francisco.
5 Sam picked him up *for* / *to* lunch.

G	E	T	O	F	F	P	T	D	D	M
G	E	T	O	U	T	O	F	R	V	I
X	B	Q	I	P	F	L	D	O	I	S
F	O	M	C	G	L	G	U	P	R	S
F	P	P	V	H	U	O	Z	O	G	D
C	E	I	R	B	A	A	L	F	E	B
A	L	F	C	O	G	N	R	F	T	G
T	A	G	T	K	P	E	G	P	I	E
C	D	E	J	C	U	O	C	E	N	T
H	G	M	H	A	S	P	Z	F	T	O
J	U	T	A	K	E	Y	A	D	O	N

B   **Complete the travel blog with *for* or *to*.**

TRIP OF A LIFETIME 🌍 🌍 🌍 🌍 ✈

I'm at the airport in Guadalajara. We're getting ready ¹_____ our trip to
Monterrey. I'm looking at a map of the city ²_____ find our hotel. It's not
far from *Barrio Antiguo*. When we get there, we plan to take a taxi, check in to the
hotel, leave our suitcases in the room, and go out ³_____ dinner.

They're calling on the passengers to board the plane. Julia is buying some snacks
⁴_____ the flight, because they don't give us food on the plane. I'm
getting in line ⁵_____ be one of the first people to board. I'm looking in
my bag ⁶_____ find my ticket. Here it is!

3 GRAMMAR AND VOCABULARY

A   **Choose the correct answers about transportation.**

1 My friend and I drive together to work. She _____ in the mornings.
   a takes a bus   b picks me up   c rides a train

2 We can't fly straight from here to Mexico City. We _____ in Miami.
   a change planes   b get out   c miss the flight

3 When I'm late, I _____ a taxi. It's faster.
   a get on   b pick up   c take

4 My friend drives a school bus. He _____ off the kids at school every morning.
   a drops   b gets   c takes

5 This traffic is so bad. I hope I don't _____ my plane.
   a catch   b change   c miss

B   **Write about a trip you took when you used different types of transportation.**

_____

_____

_____

_____

THAT'S A GREAT IDEA!

1 FUNCTIONAL LANGUAGE: Giving advice and making suggestions

A **Write the phrases from the box in the correct category.**

| how about going | perfect | that would be great | that's a great idea |
| why don't you go | ~~you could take a taxi~~ | you should take | |

Making suggestions	Agreeing
you could take a taxi	

2 REAL-WORLD STRATEGY: Echo questions

A **Complete the conversation using the echo questions in the box.**

| how long | how often | what time | where |

A Here's your key. Breakfast starts at 7:00 a.m. tomorrow.

B Sorry, [1]_____ ?

A At 7:00 a.m. Is there anything else I can do for you?

B Yes, please. I need to be downtown at 10:00 a.m. tomorrow.

A Sorry, you are going [2]_____ ?

B Downtown.

A A shuttle leaves from the hotel and goes downtown every hour.

B The shuttle leaves [3]_____ ?

A Every hour.

B Thanks. And, how long does it take to get downtown?

A Usually about 30 minutes.

B I'm sorry, it takes [4]_____ ?

A About 30 minutes.

B Great! Thanks so much.

3 FUNCTIONAL LANGUAGE AND REAL-WORLD STRATEGY

A   **Match the conversation with the correct response.**

1   I need to get to the airport tomorrow at 4:00 p.m.

2   It takes about 40 minutes to get there.

3   Where can I get souvenirs around here?

4   You need to take a taxi. It's faster.

5   Why don't you go to Brio? It's a great Italian restaurant in the mall.

a   Excuse me, how long?

b   Well, how about going to the mall around the corner?

c   That's a great idea. I don't want to be late.

d   Sorry, when did you say, sir?

e   Perfect! Where's the mall?

B   **Continue the conversation below.**

A   Where can I get souvenirs around here?

B   _____

A   _____

B   _____

A   _____

B   _____

A   _____

B   _____

A   _____

B   _____

A   _____

B   _____

A   _____

B   _____

8.4 LEAVING HOME

1 LISTENING

A 🔊 **8.01** Listen to a radio show and some answers to problems international students often have in the United States. Number the advice in the order you hear it.

_____ find a better home

_____ learn the language

_____ get to know people

_____ find out about the holidays

_____ find out about transportation

2 READING

A Read the script, and (circle) the correct answers.

▶ **Yourvideo**   Profile   Channels   Sign out

Hi! I'm Silvie. Thanks for watching my Yourvideo channel. Many of you asked me to make a video about things that we international students at American colleges need to know. Well, here's my answer.

Here are five students from other countries giving advice on things every foreign student should know about living in the US for the first time.

Keila: If your flight is more than ten hours, you may feel tired the first week of class. So bring lots of water and coffee to school.

João: Make friends before vacation starts. Everybody goes home, and you don't want to be alone at school watching everyone's social media sites. Believe me.

Farid: Don't be surprised by how much food they give you here. Remember, it's a lot, but the food is delicious, too!

Antonio: It's OK if you don't know much about popular movies or art. You can always laugh a little and look it up later on the internet.

Kim: It's OK if you don't talk to your parents every day, because when they are up during the day and free to call you, you're not!

Let me just say, don't worry too much and have fun! Let me know what you think. And if you like the video – sign up!

---

1 Who made this video?

   a a teacher   **b** a student   **c** a parent

2 After a long trip, it's normal to feel _____ the first days of school.

   a tired   **b** surprised   **c** worried

3 Why should people make friends before vacation?

   a So they can ask for help.   **b** So they are not alone during vacation.

   c So they can study together.

4 For some students, it's normal not to talk to their parents every day because of _____.

   a food differences   **b** time differences   **c** language differences

5 What advice does Silvie give at the end of her video?

   a don't be alone   **b** study hard   **c** don't worry

3 WRITING

A **Read the comments by the international students again. Write responses to them. Use the phrases in the box.**

> How about …
> I think it's a good idea …
> That's a great idea!
> I really like the idea of …
> I think it's also very important …
> You could also offer …

To Keila:

I think it's a good idea to drink lots of water when you feel tired after a long flight.

To João:

To Farid:

To Antonio:

To Kim:

B **Write suggestions for international students at your school or in your hometown. What advice can you give them?**

CHECK AND REVIEW

Read the statements. Can you do these things?

UNIT 8	Mark the boxes. ☑ I can do it. ？ I am not sure. I can …	If you are not sure, go back to these pages in the Student's Book.
VOCABULARY	☐ use words related to traveling. ☐ use verbs to talk about transportation.	page 76 page 78
GRAMMAR	☐ use *if* and *when* to talk about travel preferences. ☐ use *to* and *for* to give reasons.	page 77 page 79
FUNCTIONAL LANGUAGE	☐ give advice and make suggestions. ☐ use echo questions to ask for repetition.	page 80 page 81
SKILLS	☐ write a comment giving advice. ☐ use specific phrases to give advice.	page 83 page 83

LOOKING GOOD

WHAT TO WEAR AT WORK

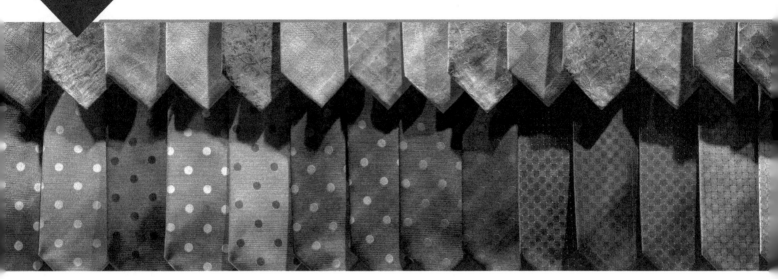

1 VOCABULARY: Naming accessories

A **Match the accessories to their uses.**

1	scarf	**a**	_____	wear on your hands
2	socks	**b**	_____	hang from your ears
3	earrings	**c**	_____	wear on your arm
4	gloves	**d**	_____	holds your pants up
5	sunglasses	**e**	_____	hang from your neck
6	belt	**f**	1	cover your neck
7	sneakers	**g**	_____	wear with a suit
8	bracelets	**h**	_____	cover your eyes
9	necklace	**i**	_____	cover your feet
10	tie	**j**	_____	wear to play basketball

2 GRAMMAR: Comparative adjectives

A **Write the adjectives under the correct category.**

~~attractive~~	cheap	cold	cool	expensive
friendly	important	interesting	warm	

More	-er
attractive	

B **Circle the correct words to complete the sentences.**

1 I wear *attractiver / more attractive* jewelry when I go to the theater.
2 That jacket is *more warm / warmer* than this one.
3 It's not possible to know if one person is *more interesting / interestinger* than another one.
4 That car is more expensive *that / than* my truck.
5 People are *more nice / nicer* around here.
6 Food at this store is *cheaper / more cheap* than at that other store.

3 GRAMMAR AND VOCABULARY

A **Complete the sentences based on the information in the chart. Each accessory is rated from 1–5. Five is the highest score.**

	Gloves	Earrings	Necklaces	Scarves	Socks
price	✓✓✓	✓✓✓✓	✓✓✓✓✓	✓✓✓	✓✓
warm	✓✓✓✓	✓	✓	✓✓✓	✓✓✓
fashionable	✓✓✓	✓✓✓✓	✓✓✓✓✓	✓✓✓	✓
quality	✓✓✓	✓✓✓✓✓	✓✓✓✓	✓✓✓✓	✓✓✓✓
importance	✓✓✓✓	✓✓✓	✓✓	✓	✓✓✓✓✓
attractive	✓✓	✓✓✓	✓✓✓	✓✓✓	✓

1 Necklaces are more important than _____scarves_____ .
2 Earrings are more fashionable than _____ .
3 Gloves are cheaper than _____ .
4 Scarves are better quality than _____ .
5 _____ are more attractive than socks.
6 _____ are warmer than scarves.

B **Write similar comparisons using the other information in exercise A.**

_____   _____
_____   _____
_____   _____

1 VOCABULARY: Describing appearance

A **Look at the clues, and complete the crossword.**

Across:

b ...

p ... e ...

m ...

l .... hair

Down:

c ... g ... hair

b ...

d ... s ... hair

2 GRAMMAR: Superlative adjectives

A **Use superlatives to complete the sentences.**

1   It is a very nice room. It is the _____nicest_____ in the hotel.

2   It is a very cheap restaurant. It is the _____ in town.

3   I am so happy. It is the _____ day of my life.

4   It's a very expensive painting. It is the _____ in the art show.

5   Spring is a very busy time for me. It is the _____ time of the year.

6   This is a very difficult class. It is the _____ class I have right now.

B **Complete the sentences with the correct form of the adjectives in parentheses.**

1 We stayed at the _____cheapest_____ (cheap) hotel in town.
2 The United States is very large, but Russia is the _____ (large) country in the world.
3 We had a great time. It was one of the _____ (amazing) vacations of our lives.
4 He is the _____ (famous) actor in movies today.
5 It's so hot out there! This is the _____ (warm) day of the summer.
6 These shoes are the _____ (fashionable) shoes of this season.

3 GRAMMAR AND VOCABULARY

A **Think about your friends, family, and famous people. Write the name of a person who …**

is tall / in your family	
has curly hair / family or friend	
dresses nice / in your school	
has beautiful eyes / a famous person	
has a beard / person you know	
looks good with a mustache	

B **Use superlative adjectives to write sentences about the information from exercise A.**

1 _____
2 _____
3 _____
4 _____
5 _____
6 _____

WHAT DO YOU THINK OF THIS?

1 FUNCTIONAL LANGUAGE: Asking for opinions

A Write the phrases in the correct category.

Do you think it's kind of bright?	~~Do you like it?~~	How do you feel about it?
I guess.	I'm not sure.	I prefer the other one.
Isn't it nice?	I think this one doesn't match.	It looks bad.
It's perfect.	What do you think of it?	

Asking for an opinion	Positive opinion	Negative or neutral opinion
Do you like it?		

2 REAL-WORLD STRATEGY: Giving opinions; *I guess*

A Complete the sentences. Use the phrases in the box above to help you. Then match the question to the best answer.

1 Are these gloves fashionable?
I'm ____not sure____ .

2 Let me try the white pair. What _____ of these?

3 How _____ about leather gloves?

4 _____ I could try a green pair. Do you like green?

5 Those blue gloves are the same color as my blouse. _____! What do you think?

a _____ Hmm. I'm not sure. Isn't white a little formal?

b _____ It looks nice, but don't you think green is kind of bright?

c __1__ Well, a lot more people are wearing them now.

d _____ Oh, yes! Those go well with your blouse.

e _____ They're not bad, but do you think leather is kind of expensive?

FUNCTIONAL LANGUAGE AND REAL-WORLD STRATEGY

A Look at the pictures and write a conversation about one pair of sneakers. Use the phrases in the box.

Do you like them?	Don't you think … ?	How do you feel about … ?	I guess …
I prefer …	I think these are …	I'm not sure.	They look …
They're perfect.	What do you think of … ?		

1 A *What do you think of those sneakers?*

   B _____

   A _____

   B _____

2 A _____

   B _____

   A _____

   B _____

3 A _____

   B _____

   A _____

   B _____

1 READING: Asking for opinions

A **Read the following text that describes an advertisement and circle the correct answers.**

> A young man with sunglasses and expensive clothes is driving a blue car.
> The car is driving very fast on a beautiful open road, in the woods.
> Now there is a second car. It's red. Both cars want to be the first one to
> get to the next town. The driver in the blue car arrives in the town first.
> He gets out of the car and laughs. It's a beautiful day and he feels happy.

1 The advertisement is selling _____.

   a vacations   **b** sunglasses   **c** cars

2 It is a _____ ad.

   a TV   **b** radio   **c** magazine

3 In the ad, what is the most important idea about the car?

   a what color it is   **b** how fast it goes   **c** how big it is

4 Who is the advertisement selling to?

   a families   **b** teenagers   **c** adults

5 What is the message behind the advertisement?

   a Blue is better than red.   **b** This is the best car to buy.   **c** It is good to be a safe driver.

2 LISTENING

A 🔊 **9.01** **Listen to the radio advertisement and circle the correct words to complete the sentences.**

1 The advertisement is about a special *model car / car sale*.

2 The car company has *hundreds / thousands* of cars to sell.

3 The sale will last for only a *weekend / a week*.

4 The sale price is *half / hundreds* off the regular price.

5 The company has *only a few / many different* types of cars to choose from.

6 The company is waiting for you to *take home a car / see their car show*.

B 🔊 **9.01** **Listen to the radio advertisement again. Does the advertisement make you want to go there? Write about why you do or don't want to buy a car from this company.**

3 WRITING

A **Rewrite the advertisement text using the correct punctuation and capitalization.**

when everythings in the right place you cant go wrong thats why the newest model from August Car Company makes it easy to choose the August Classic you can drive it in the city or you can take it on the open road you can seat up to eight people in it and feel safe its the perfect way to get comfortable with the new science behind today's cars this is the new August Classic.

its your kind of car learn more at August.com

B **Write the text for an advertisement based on the following product description.**

- The Lemon 16.4 is the most useful car of all time.
- The Lemon is the smallest city car with two doors. It is only 8.5 feet long.
- You can easily drive up to two people, and you can park almost anywhere. It is the perfect mix of space and size.
- The Lemon comes in many colors – black, red, and blue. It costs less than other cars on the market.

CHECK AND REVIEW

Read the statements. Can you do these things?

UNIT 9	Mark the boxes. ☑ I can do it. [?] I am not sure.	If you are not sure, go back to these pages in the Student's Book.
	I can ...	
VOCABULARY	☐ use words for fashion accessories.	page 86
	☐ talk about people's appearance.	page 88
GRAMMAR	☐ compare things using adjectives.	page 87
	☐ use superlative adjectives.	page 89
FUNCTIONAL LANGUAGE	☐ ask for, and give, an opinion.	page 90
	☐ use *I guess* when I'm not sure.	page 91
SKILLS	☐ write a commercial.	page 93
	☐ use uppercase letters, punctuation, and contraction apostrophes.	page 93

10.1 DANGER ON THE JOB

1 VOCABULARY: Describing jobs

A **Find the words in the box in the word search.**

accountant	architect	call center worker	dentist
engineer	IT specialist	lawyer	mechanic
nurse	paramedic	photographer	~~physical therapist~~
police officer	project manager	receptionist	

P	P	H	Y	S	I	C	A	L	T	H	E	R	A	P	I	S	T
R	P	H	O	T	O	G	R	A	P	H	E	R	O	V	R	F	V
O	F	K	D	I	M	E	C	H	A	N	I	C	R	T	X	S	J
J	E	P	A	R	A	M	E	D	I	C	P	E	K	P	T	F	C
E	B	G	G	P	J	C	R	E	F	V	B	R	G	M	I	I	P
C	D	G	I	K	L	T	R	U	C	A	P	F	C	C	T	X	A
T	B	U	O	F	M	L	E	S	N	W	L	F	S	A	S	V	C
M	I	F	X	Z	L	J	C	I	R	C	A	D	V	R	P	O	C
A	W	V	K	G	L	O	E	F	E	P	W	Z	E	C	E	N	O
N	R	A	X	S	K	T	P	V	N	A	Y	A	H	H	C	U	U
A	Q	X	N	T	C	N	T	C	G	M	E	K	L	I	I	R	N
G	P	U	R	U	U	D	I	H	I	O	R	H	E	T	A	S	T
E	G	V	J	C	I	K	O	G	N	P	U	J	F	E	L	E	A
R	S	O	L	L	G	Z	N	H	E	Z	O	B	T	C	I	B	N
I	R	L	A	M	L	X	I	R	E	Y	Q	O	V	T	S	N	T
L	O	D	E	N	T	I	S	T	R	I	E	Y	C	W	T	K	G
C	A	L	L	C	E	N	T	E	R	W	O	R	K	E	R	F	G
Q	U	P	O	L	I	C	E	O	F	F	I	C	E	R	W	U	Z

2 GRAMMAR: *have to*

A **Use *have / has* to and the best verb to complete the sentence. Use the negative when necessary.**

1 Mechanics _____ *have to repair* _____ cars.

2 A photographer _____ a camera.

3 A paramedic _____ inside a hospital.

4 An accountant _____ numbers.

5 Dentists _____ people with broken legs.

6 Call center workers _____ on the telephone.

B **Correct the sentences below.**

1 What kind of emergencies you have to help with?

<u>What kind of emergencies do you have to help with?</u>

2 I haven't to write a new software program.

_____

3 A receptionist hasn't to stand up all day.

_____

4 When have photographers to talk to actors?

_____

5 Call center workers haven't to make long business calls.

_____

6 Do you have to doing anything dangerous in your work?

_____

3 GRAMMAR AND VOCABULARY

A **Look at the information in the schedule. Write sentences about what the restaurant staff has to do each day.**

	Mon	Tue	Wed
Paul (server)	Serve food	Serve drinks and dessert	Serve food
Ray (chef)	Test new desserts	Write a new dinner menu	Buy vegetables and meat
Sam (owner)	Send emails to customers	Write a new dinner menu	Hire new server
Mica (server)	Serve food	Welcome customers	Serve food

1 <u>Paul and Mica have to serve food on Monday and Wednesday.</u>

2 _____

3 _____

4 _____

5 _____

10.2 DON'T WORRY, DAD

1 VOCABULARY: Describing health problems

A **Choose the correct verb to complete the sentence. Change the verb into the simple past.**

1 I _____ (break / cut) my finger with a knife.
2 I _____ (catch /feel) a cold. I'm sneezing a lot.
3 I _____ (break / twist) my leg when I was on vacation.
4 I _____ (have / feel) stressed last week. I had too much work.
5 I fell over yesterday and _____ (twist / cut) my ankle. Now I can't walk.
6 Ouch! I just _____ (bang / break) my head on the desk.
7 I _____ (have / catch) a headache when I woke up this morning.
8 I _____ (catch / have) a fever last week. I stayed home for 3 days.

2 GRAMMAR: Making predictions

A **Complete the sentences with the words in the box.**

may	maybe	might	probably	will	won't

1 I have to return the book I borrowed, so I _____ go to the library tomorrow.
2 I think she _____ be OK.
3 I'm not sure, but _____ he won't win the race. The other runners are very fast.
4 With all those courses, I think you will _____ feel very stressed at the end of the year.
5 I _____ fail this exam. I studied hard, so I know for sure that I will pass this time!
6 I _____ not be the best-looking person, but I'm the best actor.

B **Write the phrases from the box in the correct category.**

Do you think	I'll probably	It might be	Maybe it'll	Perhaps
What will	Will this	Will you	Won't	You'll

Ask about the future	Express future possibility	Express future plans

3 GRAMMAR AND VOCABULARY

A **Read the situations and make predictions about them using the language from exercise 2B.**

1 Bobby has a cold. He didn't study enough and feels very stressed about the math test.
   Bobby might not pass his test.

2 Many couples are having babies today. The hospital is already full, and Dr. Mills has a very busy morning.

3 Angela woke up late. She cut her finger making breakfast. She has to go to the doctor.

4 Kevin twisted his ankle at basketball practice. The final game of the year is tomorrow. His team needs him for the game.

5 Eva had a job interview yesterday. She was late, and she wore sneakers and jeans.

6 It's Lara's birthday today. She asked her parents for a dog. Last night she heard strange noises in the yard.

7 Marco is walking home in the rain. He forgot his umbrella, and missed the bus.

8 Daniel bought a ring for his girlfriend. Tonight he's taking her to a romantic restaurant for dinner.

1 FUNCTIONAL LANGUAGE: Describing a medical problem and asking for help

A Label the phrases according to their use: (O) offering help, (I) asking for information, (H) asking someone for help, or (S) describing symptoms.

1 What's wrong?   I

2 My chest hurts.   _____

3 Can you get me my medicine?   _____

4 How can I help?   _____

5 I need a towel.   _____

6 What's the matter?   _____

7 It hurts to walk.   _____

8 I have a pain in my back.   _____

9 Should I call a doctor?   _____

10 What happened?   _____

11 What do you want me to do?   _____

12 Where exactly does it hurt?   _____

2 REAL-WORLD STRATEGY: *It's like / It feels like*

A Find **three** places in the conversation where you can use *It's like or It feels like*.

A How can I help you today?

B I don't feel well. My head is killing me.

A How strong is your headache?

B Someone is hitting my head with a book.

A How do your eyes feel?

B They hurt. My eyes are on fire.

A Any other symptoms?

B My fingers are numb. I don't have my fingers.

A OK, let me look at you.

FUNCTIONAL LANGUAGE AND REAL-WORLD STRATEGY

A   Look at the pictures. Write a caption for each situation. Use an expression that matches the text in parentheses.

(Offering help)

(Asking for information about the problem)

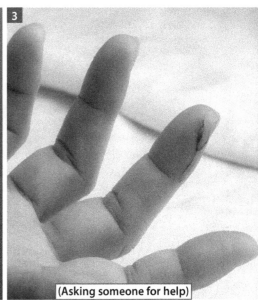

(Asking someone for help)

How can I help you?

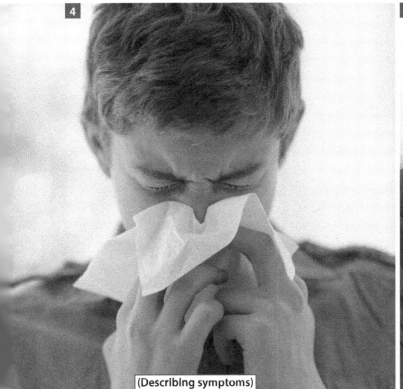

(Describing symptoms)

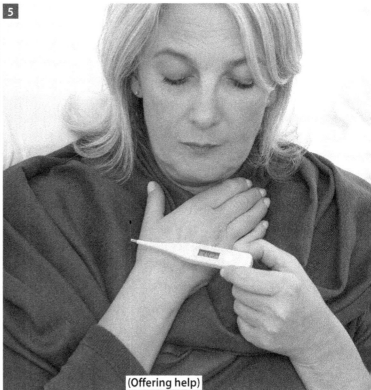

(Offering help)

1 READING

A **Read the letter and answer the questions.**

> Dear Max,
>
> I'm the teaching program manager, and we are excited to have you join us. Tomorrow you'll fly to South Africa! For two years, you will stay in a village near Cape Town. You'll teach the children in the small school there. This work is very important, so be proud of yourself. Very few people spend two years of their lives after college helping poor people.
>
> You will be away from home for a long time, so you might want to bring some music and books. And you're going to miss your family, so bring photos. It's important to remember them. Also, don't forget your medicine, you will need it.
>
> I'll meet you at the airport in Cape Town in a few days. Please email me any time you have questions.
>
> Good luck!
>
> Tom Princeton

1 Who is writing this letter?
   a Max's teacher   b Max's relative   c Max's boss
2 Where is Max going?
   a Europe   b Asia   c Africa
3 What is Max doing for the next two years?
   a studying   b teaching   c sightseeing
4 What should Max be ready for?
   a missing his family   b working a lot   c living in a city

2 LISTENING

A 🔊 **10.01 Listen to the video message and number the sentences or paragraphs in the order you hear them.**

Welcome!

_____ Please read the files and documents that our staff gave you.

_____ Finally, I'll be available to answer all the questions you might have.

_____ I'm the manager of the Helping Hands program for this country.

_____ Good luck, and enjoy your time here!

_____ I want to thank you for coming. Our team is very excited to have you with us.

_____ But you have to stay healthy.

_____ Tomorrow you will start working at our medical station.

_____ The work you will do in the next few weeks is very important, but it is also dangerous. Many people need our help.

_____ Please remember to have your ID and your cell phone with you at all times.

B 🔊 **10.01** **Listen to the video message again and write the number of each sentence in the correct category.**

Introduction	Giving advice	Positive ending

3 WRITING

A **Complete the email with your own answers. Add *anyway* and *by the way*.**

Reply Forward

Hey Ivan,

My name is ¹_____, and I heard you are joining our English class. That's great.
²_____, the ³_____ is excellent and the class is really fun.
⁴_____, you've missed two lessons, so, let me give you some advice about
the things we did in those classes. The last topic we covered was ⁵_____.
For homework, ⁶_____.
During class, ⁷_____.
After class, ⁸_____.
I hope this helps you have a good start. Let me know if you have any other questions.
Take care,
⁹_____

CHECK AND REVIEW

Read the statements. Can you do these things?

UNIT 10	Mark the boxes. ☑ I can do it. ❓ I am not sure. I can ...	If you are not sure, go back to these pages in the Student's Book.
VOCABULARY	☐ use words to describe jobs. ☐ use words to describe health problems.	page 98 page 100
GRAMMAR	☐ use *have to* to talk about things that are necessary. ☐ make predictions about the future with *will*.	page 99 page 101
FUNCTIONAL LANGUAGE	☐ describe a medical problem and ask for help. ☐ use *it's like* and *it feels like* to describe a problem.	page 102 page 103
SKILLS	☐ write a letter of advice. ☐ use *anyway* and *by the way*.	page 105 page 105

1 VOCABULARY: Using verb-noun internet phrases

A Write ten verb-noun phrases with the words below.

add someone		app
build		friend
change		group
check	a	link
click	an	messages
join	as a	social media account
make	on a	password
message	your	right
open		someone
swipe		video

1 add someone as a friend

2 _____

3 _____

4 _____

5 _____

6 _____

7 _____

8 _____

9 _____

10 _____

2 GRAMMAR: Present perfect for experience

A Complete the chart with the present perfect form of the verbs.

Simple present	Present perfect
be	have been
build	
do	
have	
join	
make	
message	

B   **Correct the sentences.**

1   She have build hundreds of websites. _____

2   Have you ever were to Japan? _____

3   Has they change their passwords? _____

4   I don't have checked my messages. _____

5   He have added me as a friend. _____

3   GRAMMAR AND VOCABULARY

A   **Write questions using present perfect. Use the answers to help you.**

1   A   *Have you ever been outside the country?* _____
     B   No, I've never been outside the country.

2   A   _____
     B   No, they've never built an app.

3   A   _____
     B   Yes, I've made two videos with my friends.

4   A   _____
     B   No, I've never added someone I don't know as a friend.

5   A   _____
     B   No, she's never messaged a famous person.

6   A   _____
     B   Yes, he has changed his password!

7   A   _____
     B   Yes, she's written three songs.

8   A   _____
     B   Yes, they've lived in a different country.

9   A   _____
     B   No, he hasn't found a job.

10   A   _____
     B   Yes, I've checked my messages.

SOCIAL MEDIA LIKES

1 VOCABULARY: Using social media verbs

A **Make words from the letters.**

1 dloadwno ___download___   6 rofacehrs _____
2 wollfo _____   7 iekl _____
3 agilorv _____   8 kcobl _____
4 rkmoobak _____   9 nigol _____
5 olpuda _____   10 arshe _____

B (Circle) **the correct options to complete the sentences.**

1 Have you ever *uploaded / gone viral* photos of your friends to a social media site?
2 Catherine *searched / followed* for a new coat online.
3 The video of Paula and Rajesh's wedding party *liked / went viral*. You have to see the dancing!
4 Last night I *blocked / downloaded* the English class assignment. I needed to study it.
5 Have you ever *logged in / shared* to that website where you can see your house?
6 There is a problem with that website. I tried to open it, but my computer *blocked / liked* it.

2 GRAMMAR: Present perfect and simple past

A **Read the sentences. Then write a question about each one in the simple past.**

1 I've downloaded this great app.   When ___did you download it___ ?
2 I've uploaded some photos onto my Facebook page.   When _____ ?
3 She's blocked her ex-boyfriend.   Why _____ ?
4 I've lost my phone.   Where _____ ?
5 We've met so many interesting people.   Where _____ ?
6 He's found an old friend from ten years ago on Facebook.   How _____ ?

B   Complete the text with the correct form of the verbs in parentheses. Look up the past participle of the verbs if you need to.

Have I ever ¹_____*lost*_____ (lose) my phone? Yes, I have. I ²_____
(lose) it on the bus last week, but someone ³_____ (find) it and I got it
back. But I ⁴_____ (never break) my phone. My sister ⁵_____
(break) three phones! The last time, she was in the kitchen and she ⁶_____
(drop) it into the tomato sauce. She ⁷_____ (clean) it, but it
didn't help. Yesterday, she ⁸_____ (buy) her fourth phone.

3 GRAMMAR AND VOCABULARY

A   Write questions using the verbs and phrases with the present perfect.

1   (eat) most expensive restaurant   *What is the most expensive restaurant you've ever eaten in?*
2   (be) in a video   _____
3   (study) Japanese   _____
4   (walk) far in one day   _____
5   (forget) the birthday of someone important _____
6   (receive) best gift   _____
7   (take) funniest photo   _____
8   (cook) for a lot of people   _____

B   Write your answers to the questions in exercise A.

1   *Gina's Italian Restaurant in Rio is the most expensive restaurant I've ever eaten in.*
2   _____
3   _____
4   _____
5   _____
6   _____
7   _____
8   _____

CAN I USE YOUR PHONE?

1 FUNCTIONAL LANGUAGE: Making and responding to requests

A **Write the phrases in the box in the correct category.**

| Can I | Could you | I'm afraid not | No, I'm sorry |
| No problem | Would you mind | Yeah, that's fine | |

Making requests	Accepting requests	Refusing requests

2 REAL-WORLD STRATEGY: Remembering words

A **Complete the conversations using the questions in the box.**

| What do you call … | What do you call … | What's his/her … | What's it … |

A Hi, do you need any help?

B Hi, yes. Do you mind taking a look at my … [1]_____ called?

A Your tablet? No problem.

B Thanks. I downloaded a video yesterday, and now I can't open my …
[2]_____ it?

A Your email?

B Yes, my email. Could you take a look, please?

A Wow, she's beautiful! [3]_____ name?

B Her name is Felicity Jones.

A Is she a … [4]_____ it?

B An actor? Yes, she's a movie star.

A Awesome!

3 FUNCTIONAL LANGUAGE AND REAL-WORLD STRATEGY

A **Read the situations below and choose one. You will write a conversation asking for help. Before you write the conversation, complete the chart with expressions you plan to use.**

You are a tourist. Ask someone for a good restaurant in town.

You are lost in a new city. Ask someone to give you directions.

Asking someone to do something	
Accepting requests	
Refusing requests	
Remembering words	

B **Write your conversation with the expressions from exercise A.**

A Hi. _____ ?

B _____

A _____

B _____

A _____

B _____

A _____

B _____

1 READING

A   Read the magazine article. Then read the sentences and write *T* if true or *F* if false. Then write true sentences for the false ones.

HOW TO TAKE AMAZING SELFIES!

Love to take selfies, but hate the way they look? Here are some simple tips to look your best and have amazing selfies!

TIP 1   Light is your most important friend. How often have your photos looked too dark? Could you go outside or stand near a window to take your selfie? That's much better. You'll look so beautiful!

TIP 2   What's behind you? Is it an exciting place or only your face? If you hold the camera too close, your nose looks very big! Can we fix that? No problem! Hold your phone far away, and use the zoom. Then your face will look normal.

TIP 3   Wear fun accessories like sunglasses, a big hat, or a scarf. Make your selfies interesting!

TIP 4   Laugh! Be happy and you'll have an amazing selfie!

1 _____ This article is about how to dress better.

_____

2 _____ The article says it's difficult to take selfies outside.

_____

3 _____ The article explains why your nose may look too big in selfies.

_____

4 _____ The writer doesn't know how to solve the problem of big noses in selfies.

_____

5 _____ The writer thinks wearing hats make selfies boring.

_____

6 _____ The writer probably likes happy selfies best.

_____

2 LISTENING

A   🔊 **11.01** Listen to the conversation. Then ⬭circle the correct answers.

1 Tanya is having a problem _____.

   a taking selfies   b fixing her camera   c using her social media site

2 How does Tanya describe her photos?

   a They're too light.   b They're all terrible.   c They're too dark.

3 What does Shin think will probably help Tanya's photos?

   a uploading them   b using the flash   c making them darker

4 What does Tanya ask Shin to do?

   a take photos of her   b take photos with her   c teach her how to take photos

B ◀) **11.01** **Listen to the conversation again. Then complete the sentences with phrases from the conversation.**

1 I _____have taken_____ so many selfies, and they're all terrible.

2 I've looked at the photos _____.

3 Have you used the _____ ?

4 I've _____ it.

5 Hey, _____ teaching me more about taking photos?

6 _____ Monday?

3 WRITING

A **Complete the sentences about you.**

1 I take selfies when _____

2 I never take selfies when _____

3 I share selfies with _____

4 I take selfies at _____

5 I change selfies when _____

B **Read the article about selfies again. What information is useful? Use your answers in exercise A to write about how you take selfies. Include something positive, something negative, and something that you had a different idea about before.**

_____

_____

_____

_____

_____

CHECK AND REVIEW

Read the statements. Can you do these things?

UNIT 11	Mark the boxes. ☑ I can do it. ? I am not sure. I can …	If you are not sure, go back to these pages in the Student's Book.
VOCABULARY	☐ use verb-noun internet phrases. ☐ use social media verbs.	page 108 page 110
GRAMMAR	☐ use the present perfect to talk about experience. ☐ use the present perfect and simple past to talk about what I've done and when I did it.	page 109 page 111
FUNCTIONAL LANGUAGE	☐ make and respond to requests. ☐ ask questions to remember words.	page 112 page 113
SKILLS	☐ write comments about an online article. ☐ use *I always thought …*, *I think it's interesting that …*, and *Who cares?*	page 115 page 115

1 VOCABULARY: Describing weather

A Look at the pictures and complete the crossword.

Across:

 2

 4

 5

 8

 11

 12

 13

 14

Down:

 1

 2

 3

 4

 6

 7

 9

 10

2 GRAMMAR: *be like*

A **Put the words in the correct order to make questions.**

1 the / like / What's / weather / ?
   What's the weather like?

2 course / like / will / be / the / What / ?

3 What / party / was / like / the /?

4 music / was / the / like / What / ?

5 she / younger / What / like / was / when / she / was / ?

6 be / What / the / will / teacher / like / ?

B **Match the questions in exercise A to the answers below.**

_____ The music was excellent.

_____ I heard he will be great.

__1__ It's sunny and warm.

_____ It will be hard because the textbook is very difficult.

_____ It was fun because a lot of friends came by.

_____ She was very funny and happy.

3 GRAMMAR AND VOCABULARY

A **Answer the questions with your own information. Write complete sentences.**

1 What's the weather like today?

2 What's your best friend like?

3 What was your last birthday party like?

4 What will this weekend be like for you?

5 What are your English classmates like?

THIS TRIP HAS IT ALL

1 VOCABULARY: Describing landscapes and cityscapes

A **Find the words from the box in the word search.**

cave	cliff	coast	fountain	glacier
rainforest	rocks	skyscraper	stadium	statue
stream	tower	valley	waterfall	

```
R  S  Y  R  M  I  E  L  D  Q  E  E  T  G
G  E  F  A  O  W  L  T  C  X  U  C  P  L
O  W  O  I  G  P  S  F  D  U  T  A  Y  A
X  A  U  N  M  F  H  T  J  O  A  V  C  C
D  T  N  F  A  Z  W  S  A  T  T  E  D  I
S  E  T  O  L  L  T  U  K  D  S  N  I  E
X  R  A  R  L  I  G  D  K  H  I  Z  X  R
J  F  I  E  S  T  R  E  A  M  D  U  G  F
Y  A  N  S  F  H  Y  R  H  R  W  L  M  E
B  L  G  T  S  K  Y  S  C  R  A  P  E  R
O  L  P  H  E  H  M  H  P  T  O  W  E  R
O  K  Q  T  T  C  L  I  F  F  D  F  N  Y
I  S  T  A  T  U  E  M  L  C  O  A  S  T
X  J  R  O  C  K  S  K  V  A  L  L  E  Y
```

B **Choose the correct answer.**

1 After a day of sightseeing in Rome, we sat by the _____ of a horse in front of the large skyscraper.
   a statue   b rocks   c waterfall
2 From the ship we could see the large white ice that formed the _____.
   a valley   b glacier   c skyscraper
3 You will often know a city when you see pictures of its _____.
   a streams   b rainforests   c skyscrapers
4 Acapulco is famous for its swimmers who jump from the _____.
   a cliffs   b caves   c towers
5 Thousands of people come to the _____ to see sports and concerts.
   a valley   b stadium   c cave
6 Some people enjoy walking through a _____ to catch fish.
   a stream   b coast   c fountain

2 GRAMMAR: Relative pronouns: *who, which, that*

A **Complete the sentences with *who, which,* or *that*.**

1 The person _____*who*_____ helps you at the store is the clerk.

2 This is the song _____ my parents danced to at their wedding.

3 This is the painting _____ makes me feel calm.

4 Those are the people _____ I spend more time with.

5 This is my friend _____ always helps when I'm in trouble.

6 It is a city _____ is fun day and night.

B **Correct the sentences.**

1 That's the person which helped me last time.

_____

2 That's the jacket who I wear almost every day.

_____

3 Those are the presents who I received last month.

_____

4 It is one place who I would really like to visit in the future.

_____

5 That's the player which scored more points in the game.

_____

3 GRAMMAR AND VOCABULARY

A **Answer the questions with your own information. Write complete sentences.**

1 Who is your friend who likes to take photos?
Jacques is a friend who likes to take photos.

_____

2 What's the TV show that you watch every day?

_____

3 What's the last book that you read?

_____

4 What's the video game which you like the most?

_____

5 What's the city that you want to visit next?

_____

6 What's the sport that you play the most?

_____

12.3 I THINK WE'RE LOST

1 FUNCTIONAL LANGUAGE: Asking for help and giving directions

A **Put the conversation in order.**

☐ Luigi's? No, you need to go back the way you came. See that store there?

☑ Hello, excuse me. We're looking for Luigi's Restaurant. Are we going in the right direction?

☐ Store? Oh, that one on the corner?

☐ Oh, dear. That's a long way.

☐ That's right! Turn right on that corner.

☐ OK, we turn right, and then what?

☐ Thanks. We'll try walking.

☐ Then walk for 15 minutes down the street, and you'll see Luigi's on the left.

☐ You can also take the bus on the corner. It comes every 30 minutes.

2 REAL-WORLD STRATEGY: Correcting yourself

A **Use the words in the box to correct the statements.**

> No, wait …   Well, actually …

1 The Eiffel Tower is in New York City.   Well, actually, the Eiffel Tower is in Paris.

2 There is no water on Mars. _____

3 New Year's Eve is in June. _____

4 Tokyo is in Europe. _____

5 December is cold in Australia. _____

3 FUNCTIONAL LANGUAGE AND REAL-WORLD STRATEGY

A Look at the map below and complete the conversations with the correct phrases.

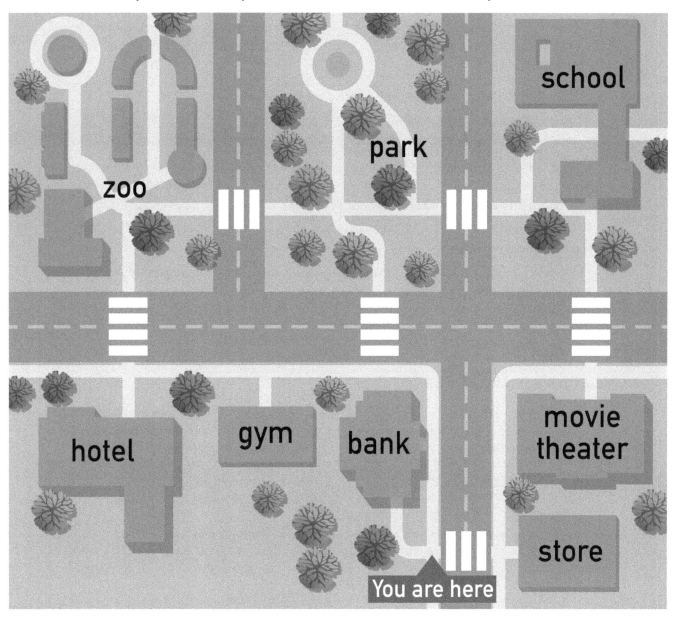

A

A Excuse me. ¹ _____ us, please? ² _____
for the school.

B ³ _____ (give directions). ⁴ _____ . (correct
yourself)

A OK. Can you show me on the map?

B ⁵ _____ . (positive response)

A Great, thanks!

B

A Excuse me, I'm looking for the hotel. ⁶ _____ ?

B ⁷ _____ . (give directions, then correct yourself)

A Thanks!

1 LISTENING

A 🔊 12.01 **Listen to the conversation and choose the correct answer.**

1 What are the friends talking about?
   a which area they like best   b the empty space on the street   c the garden growing at their house

2 In the past, the empty space was a _____.
   a city park   b school   c garden

3 Who do the friends decide to talk to about their idea?
   a the neighbors   b their parents   c some farmers

4 The friends plan to plant _____.
   a trees   b flowers   c vegetables

5 They want to start a _____.
   a farmers' market   b grocery store   c cleaning business

2 READING

A **Read the blog below and check (✓) True or False.**

> I've never been good with plants, but I moved to a new apartment that's not very big, and decided I needed a wall garden. Why? Well, plants are beautiful to look at and they help clean the air. A wall garden is a way that a lot of plants can grow without taking too much floor space.
>
> It's not very easy to grow a wall garden. You have to make sure it's not too heavy, and that it gets enough light. Also, you have to make sure you don't give it too much water. Then the plants get yellow and their leaves fall off.
>
> The most important thing for a beautiful wall garden is plant food. Put some in the water every month, and you will have awesome green plants. It's the best thing I've ever done!

	True	False
1 Large plants will fit in the writer's apartment.	☐	☐
2 The writer has always been good with plants.	☐	☐
3 Wall gardens need good planning.	☐	☐
4 The most important thing is to water the plants very often.	☐	☐
5 The writer is happy with the garden.	☐	☐

3 WRITING

A **Use the words in the box to complete the instructions.**

Finally	First	Next	Now	Then

Five Steps to Food from the Garden to Your Table: Grow Your Own Salad!

1 _____, go to your local store and buy seeds for lettuce, tomatoes, onions, and other salad favorites.

2 _____, make sure you have space for each type of plant.

3 _____, plant your seeds in a sunny place and water them twice a week.

4 _____ watch your plants grow.

5 _____, get your lettuce, a tomato, and an onion from the garden. Wash them, and enjoy your fresh salad!

B **Write five steps to selling your vegetables at a farmers' market. Use the phrases in the box.**

choose the vegetables	get the vegetables from the garden	sell your vegetables
wash the vegetables	write the price	

1 _____

2 _____

3 _____

4 _____

5 _____

CHECK AND REVIEW

Read the statements. Can you do these things?

UNIT 12	Mark the boxes. ☑ I can do it. ? I am not sure.		If you are not sure, go back to these pages in the Student's Book.
	I can …		
VOCABULARY	☐ use words to describe the weather.		page 118
	☐ use words to talk about landscapes and cityscapes.		page 120
GRAMMAR	☐ ask and answer questions with *be like*.		page 119
	☐ use *who, which,* and *that* to give information about people and things.		page 121
FUNCTIONAL LANGUAGE	☐ ask for help and give directions.		page 122
	☐ correct myself.		page 123
SKILLS	☐ write simple, short instructions.		page 125
	☐ use sequencing words.		page 125

EXTRA ACTIVITIES

1   TIME TO SPEAK   Things you have in common

A   **Find out about things you have in common with your friends and family.**

- Write some questions. See examples below:

  When is your birthday?

  How many brothers and sisters do you have?

  What city are your parents from?

  Where are your grandparents from?

- Add more questions to the list above.
- Post the questions to your social media account, or email them to friends and family.
- Create a private group and invite your friends and family members.

B   **Ask your friends and family to answer the questions. Make a list of things that you have in common with them.**

2   TIME TO SPEAK   Apps for life

A   **Write an app review.**

- Look at the apps on your phone.
- Make a list of the three apps that you use the most.
- Select your favorite out of the three.
- Write: 1) what is good and not so good about that app, 2) how the app helps you with your daily life, 3) what changes you want to see in future versions. Use the expressions from the unit to express your opinions and give examples.
- Go to an app store and find the app's page.
- Write a review of the app using your ideas.

3   TIME TO SPEAK   Fitness programs

A   **Choose a couple of gyms or sports clubs that you know of or like. Go online. Find out about their fitness programs. Compare the fitness programs in both places and decide which one is better for you. Recommend the place you selected to your classmates at the next class. Explain your reasons.**

4   TIME TO SPEAK   The gift of giving

A   **Imagine you want to give a small gift to a friend living in another country.**

- Write about what she or he likes to wear and do.
- Call her or him or contact her/him online and ask about his/her interests and hobbies.
- Make a list of possible gifts that are typical of your country or region.
- Decide what gift is the best. Think of something unusual and attractive.

B   **Make a decision about the gift for your friend and explain it in the next class.**

5 TIME TO SPEAK Iceberg!

A   Read the fact file below. Research more facts online about the life of this *Titanic* survivor.

Name	Lawrence Beesley
Birthdate	December 31, 1877
Nationality	British
Age	35 years old
Occupation	Science teacher
Author of	*The Loss of the SS Titanic*
Death	February 14, 1967
Quote	"… it was easy to lose one's way on the *Titanic*."

B   Write the story of Lawrence Beesley. Use the facts you know about him to write a short description of his life.

C   Present your story at the next class.

6 TIME TO SPEAK Eureka!

A   Go online and find an invention that you like. Find out about:
- what problem it solves.
- when it was invented.
- how much the product costs.

B   Write a report about the invention and bring it to the next class. Explain it and discuss it with the rest of the class.

7 TIME TO SPEAK The perfect party

A   Design the menu you created in class for your party. Use your own ideas, or you can find ideas online. Complete the fields with the necessary information.
- date
- event name
- menu dishes
- descriptions of the dishes

B   Find pictures of your dishes. Illustrate the menu with the pictures.

C   Bring your menu to the next class. Show it and explain it to the rest of the class.

EXTRA ACTIVITIES

8 TIME TO SPEAK Planning a trip

A **Help tourists plan their trip by writing a review for a travel website.**

- Think of a place you have visited.
- List the things you did and the places you visited there.
- Write one comment for each place or activity based on your experience.
- In each comment, make one suggestion for other travelers.
- Go to a travel website.
- Find the places on your list.
- Rate the places and create a review with your comments.

9 TIME TO SPEAK Sell it!

A **Perform the ad that you prepared in class. Record it with your phone. Show your ad to your classmates in the next class. Comment on your classmates' ads. Vote for the best ad in the class.**

10 TIME TO SPEAK Reality TV

A **Go online and search for an article about a reality show that you don't like. In the comments section, make two suggestions for how the show could be better. Think about what the contestants can do and how they can make it better. Explain why these changes will make the show better.**

11 TIME TO SPEAK Online videos

A **Go online.**

- Find a video online that you like.
- Write a comment about what happened in the video and why you liked it.
- Post your comment.

B **Now find a video that you didn't like.**

- Explain why you didn't like it in two sentences.
- Post your comment.

12 TIME TO SPEAK Places that you'll love

A **Take a picture of a beautiful outdoor area in your city or region.**

- Write a short description of the place.
- Tell about a great experience you had there.
- Go online to a travel website for tourists.
- Post your photo and your comments.

B **Wait for friends and people to comment on your post. Answer the comments.**

NOTES

The authors and publishers acknowledge the following sources of copyright material and are grateful for the permissions granted. While every effort has been made, it has not always been possible to identify the sources of all the material used, or to trace all copyright holders. If any omissions are brought to our notice, we will be happy to include the appropriate acknowledgements on reprinting and in the next update to the digital edition, as applicable.

Photography credits
Key: B = Below, BG = Background, BL = Below Left, BR = Below Right, C = Centre, CL = Centre Left, CR = Centre Right, T = Top, TC = Top Centre, TL = Top Left, TR = Top Right.

All images are sourced from Getty Images.

p. 2 (BG): aldomurillo/E+; p. 2 (couple): Antonio_Diaz/iStock/Getty Images Plus; p. 4 (keychain): Michael Zwahlen/EyeEm; p. 4 (brush): Ghrzuzudu/iStock/Getty Images Plus; p. 4 (umbrella): macrovector/iStock/Getty Images Plus; p. 6 (BG): Caiaimage/Sam Edwards; p. 7: Westend61; p. 8: Elke Meitzel/Cultura; p. 10: T3 Magazine/Future; p. 12 (photo 1): Topic Images Inc.; p. 12 (photo 2): Shannon Fagan/DigitalVision; p. 12 (photo 3): Image Source; p. 12 (photo 4): pixhook/E+; p. 12 (photo 5): Zocha_K/E+; p. 12 (photo 6): bagi1998/E+; p. 14 (CL): Tom Grill/Photographer's Choice RF; p. 14 (CR): markgoddard/iStock/Getty Images Plus; p. 15: Caner CANDEMIR/iStock/Getty Images Plus; p. 16: Kelvin Murray/Stone; p. 18 (LED): fredrocko/E+; p. 18 (tennis player): PeopleImages/DigitalVision; p. 18 (soccer): vgajic/E+; p. 18 (field): adventtr/iStock/Getty Images Plus; p. 18 (goal): Cocoon/DigitalVision; p. 18 (court): David Madison/DigitalVision; p. 18 (race): Hero Images; p. 18 (pool): baona/iStock/Getty Images Plus; p. 18 (athlete): Milk & Honey Creative/Stone; p. 18: (fans): LeoPatrizi/E+; p. 18 (gym): XiXinXing; p. 20 (TL): alvarez/E+; p. 20 (TC): Robert Llewellyn/Photolibrary; p. 20 (TR): Ariel Skelley/DigitalVision; p. 21: gilaxia/iStock/Getty Images Plus; p. 22 (TL): Handout/Getty Images Sport; p. 22 (TR): Jeff Greenberg/Universal Images Group; p. 24: ©fitopardo.com/Moment; p. 25: Jeff Greenberg/Universal Images Group; p. 27: PeopleImages/E+; p. 28: Maximilian Stock Ltd/Photographer's Choice; p. 29 (CL): stevezmina1/DigitalVision Vectors; p. 29 (C): kimberrywood/DigitalVision Vectors; p. 29 (CR): KristinaVelickovic/DigitalVision Vectors; p. 29 (B): Dougal Waters/DigitalVision; p. 30: Peter Cade/The Image Bank; p. 31 (TL): TonySoh/DigitalVision Vectors; p. 31 (TC): nico_blue/DigitalVision Vectors; p. 31 (TR): Leontura/DigitalVision Vectors; p. 32: Jim Rankin/Toronto Star; p. 33: MIKE NELSON/AFP; p. 35: Mike Powell/DigitalVision; p. 36: Peter Dazeley/Photographer's Choice; p. 37 (TR): Pictorial Parade/Archive Photos; p. 37 (BR): Stuart Franklin – FIFA; p. 38 (T): Commercial Eye/The Image Bank; p. 38 (BR): pshonka/iStock/Getty Images Plus; p. 39 (TR): ZU_09/DigitalVision Vectors; p. 40 (BR): Marcelo Endelli/LatinContent WO; p. 40 (TR): Yadid Levy/robertharding; p. 42 (TV): Cobalt88/iStock/Getty Images Plus; p. 42 (console): Jane_Kelly/iStock/Getty Images Plus; p. 42 (sweater): Mark Murphy/DigitalVision Vectors; p. 42 (cart): johavel/iStock/Getty Images Plus; p. 46 (TR): andresr/E+; p. 46 (powerbar): LongHa2006/E+; p. 46 (BR): Yagi Studio/Taxi; p. 47 (joystick): Emanuele Ravecca/EyeEm; p. 47 (eyelash): Steve Wisbauer/Stockbyte; p. 47 (tape): sergeyskleznev/iStock/Getty Images Plus; p. 47 (pillow): ChamilleWhite/iStock/Getty Images Plus; p. 48: Roy JAMES Shakespeare/The Image Bank; p. 50 (onion): Westend61; p. 50 (avocado): Richard Coombs/EyeEm; p. 50 (strawberry): ARB/Cultura; p. 50 (lettuce): artphotoclub/iStock/Getty Images Plus; p. 50 (butter): Chee Siong Teh/EyeEm; p. 50 (chili): fotoARION - Specialist in product and business photography/Moment; p. 50 (cereal): Creative Crop/DigitalVision; p. 50 (steak): anna1311/iStock/Getty Images Plus; p. 50 (pasta): Giovanni Boscherino/EyeEm; p. 50 (noodles): Pinghung Chen/EyeEm; p. 50 (hamburger): Olga Nayashkova/Hemera/Getty Images Plus; p. 50 (jam): masahiro Makino/Moment; p. 50 (salt): Kristin Lee; p. 50 (yogurt): clubfoto/iStock/Getty Images Plus; p. 50 (pepper): GregorBister/iStock/Getty Images Plus; p. 50 (corn): photomaru/iStock/Getty Images Plus; p. 51: FatCamera/iStock/Getty Images Plus; p. 52: maikid/E+; p. 53: Spiderstock/iStock/Getty Images Plus; p. 54: GeorgeRudy/iStock/Getty Images Plus; p. 55: Jeff Greenberg/Universal Images Group; p. 58: Mlenny/E+; p. 60: chombosan/iStock/Getty Images Plus; p. 61: gazanfer/iStock/Getty Images Plus; p. 63: kzenon/iStock/Getty Images Plus; p. 64 (TR): andresr/E+; p. 64 (CL): Michael Blann/Iconica; p. 66: Piotr Powietrzynski/Photolibraryl; p. 67: Fidelis Simanjuntak/Moment; p. 68 (bald, beard & darkhair), p. 83 (icon), p. 90 (boiling, dry, lightning & rainy): bubaone/DigitalVision Vectors; p. 68 (pierced): bortonia/DigitalVision Vectors; p. 68 (mustache): madebymarco/iStock/Getty Images Plus; p. 68 (hair): AliceLiddelle/iStock/Getty Images Plus; p. 68 (curly): Sudowoodo/iStock/Getty Images Plus; p. 69: paul mansfield photography/Moment; p. 70: Daniel Limpi/EyeEm; p. 71 (TL): Daniel Diebel; p. 71 (TR): Muralinath/iStock/Getty Images Plus; p. 71 (C): Babayev/iStock/Getty Images Plus; p. 72: Bloomberg; p. 75: Wavebreakmedia/iStock/Getty Images Plus; p. 76: Anna Pekunova/Moment; p. 77: FatCamera/iStock/Getty Images Plus; p. 78: Jeff Greenberg/Universal Images Group; p. 79 (TL): PM Images/Iconica; p. 79 (TC): BSIP/Universal Images Group; p. 79 (TR): worac/iStock/Getty Images Plus; p. 79 (BL): Tetra Images; p. 79 (BR): LEA PATERSON/SCIENCE PHOTO LIBRARY; p. 80: Colin Hawkins/Stone; p. 83 (woman): Granger Wootz/Blend Images; p. 84 (like): pop_jop/DigitalVision Vectors; p. 84 (friends): Klaus Vedfelt/Taxi; p. 85 (TR): ronstik/iStock/Getty Images Plus; p. 85 (B): Image Source/DigitalVision; p. 87: KLH49/iStock/Getty Images Plus; p. 88: David Aaron Troy/Taxi; p. 90 (flood): chokkicx/DigitalVision Vectors; p. 90 (hurricane): ayvengo/iStock/Getty Images Plus; p. 90 (stormy, snowstorm & freezing): AVIcons/iStock/Getty Images Plus; p. 90 (windy): MrsWilkins/iStock/Getty Images Plus; p. 90 (foggy & humid): sabuhinovruzov/iStock/Getty Images Plus; p. 90 (thunder): JakeOlimb/DigitalVision Vectors; p. 90 (snowy): Color_life/iStock/Getty Images Plus; p. 90 (sunny): StudioBarcelona/iStock/Getty Images Plus; p. 90 (cloudy): Hilch/iStock/Getty Images Plus; p. 91: john finney photography/Moment; p. 93: Philippe Lissac/GODONG/Corbis Documentary; p. 94: VisitBritain/Grant Pritchard; p. 96: JoeLena/DigitalVision Vectors.

Front cover photography by Alija/E+/Getty Images.

Illustration
Dusan Lakicevic (Beehive illustration) p. 13; Liav Zabari (Lemonade illustration) pp. 19, 39; Martin Sanders (Beehive illustration) p. 95.

Audio
Audio production by CityVox, New York.

Corpus
Development of this publication has made use of the Cambridge English Corpus (CEC). The CEC is a multi-billion word collection of contemporary spoken and written English. It includes British English, American English, and other varieties. It also includes the Cambridge Learner Corpus, the world's biggest collection of learner writing, developed in collaboration with Cambridge Assessment. Cambridge University Press uses the CEC to provide evidence about language use that helps to produce better language teaching materials.

Our *Evolve* authors study the Corpus to see how English is really used, and to identify typical learner mistakes. This information informs the authors' selection of vocabulary, grammar items and Student's Book Corpus features such as the Accuracy Check, Register Check, and Insider English